Easy PC Presentations

Other titles by the same author
BP 508 Easy PC Digital Imaging

Other titles of interest
BP 524 How to use PowerPoint 2002
BP 509 Microsoft Office XP Explained

Easy PC Presentations

Geoff Preston

Bernard Babani (publishing) Ltd
The Grampians
Shepherds Bush Road
London W6 7NF
www.babanibooks.com

Please note

Although every care has been taken with the production of this book to ensure that any projects, designs, modifications, and/or programs etc., contained herewith, operate in a correct and safe manner and also that the components specified are normally available in Great Britain, the Publisher and Author do not accept responsibility in any way for the failure (including fault in design) of any projects, design, modification, or program to work correctly or to cause damage to any equipment that it may be connected to or used in conjunction with, or in respect of any other damage or injury that may be caused, nor do the Publishers accept responsibility in any way for the failure to obtain specified components.

Notice is also given that if any equipment that is still under warranty is modified in any way or used or connected with home-built equipment then that warranty may be void.

© BERNARD BABANI (publishing) LTD

First Published – October 2002

British Library Cataloguing in Publication Data
A catalogue record for this book is available from the British Library

ISBN 0 85934 529 7

Cover Design by Gregor Arthur
Printed and bound in Great Britain by Cox and Wyman

About this Book

It takes a great deal of nerve to stand in front of an audience and give a Presentation. If you've got the confidence to stand in front of colleagues to give a Presentation, it can be a rewarding experience. This book will help you to overcome any nerves you may have by giving you the confidence to do the job.

Each step is clearly explained so that you can confidently research, prepare and deliver a professional Presentation.

Although you may present your talk unaided, this book explains how to prepare a computerised presentation to accompany your talk. Although the explanations refer to Microsoft's Powerpoint, similar presentations can be created in a variety of alternative applications and some of these are also outlined in the book.

Trademarks

All brand and product names used in this book are recognised trademarks, or registered trademarks of their respective companies. There is no intent to use any trademarks generically and readers should investigate ownership of a trademark before using it for any purpose.

Acknowledgements

Thanks to Atomwide Ltd, GeoTAB, SfE and Trust Ltd for supplying hardware and software and for providing help and support during the production of this book.

About the Author

Geoff Preston trained as a Technology teacher in the mid 1970's, specialising in Technical Graphics, but soon became involved with computers when the Government of the day began providing them for schools.

He took up a teaching appointment as Head of Information Technology at a North London secondary school where he worked for 11 years. During this time he developed one of the first school networks covering the entire school site.

He has written about educational ICT issues in numerous magazines, and for 7 years was the Education Editor for a popular computer magazine.

In 1996 he was appointed Consultant Editor for InteracTive Magazine and has since been a regular contributor.

Easy PC Presentations draws on his experiences as a successful teacher and lecturer. He is an acknowledged authority on portable computing, local area networks and the Internet, and has written widely on these subjects as well as having published numerous best-selling books.

Contents

1

Introduction 1

Overhead projector — 3
Computer — 4
Where can it be used? — 5
   Accompany a talk of lecture — 5
   Standalone display — 6
   Interactive learning module — 7
Conventions used in this book — 8

2

Planning 9

What first? — 9
What type of presentation? — 9
Who is your audience — 10
   How many are coming? — 10
   Who will be there? — 10
   Why will they be there? — 11
   What will they know? — 11
The Location — 11
   How do I get there? — 11
   Is it worth staying in a hotel? — 11
   What type of venue is it? — 11
   What are the audio qualities? — 11
   What visual aids are there? — 11
About the Presentation — 13
   How long? — 13
   When is the start? — 13
   How many speakers? — 13
   Who will they be? — 13
   Will there be questions? — 13

Is there a dress code?	14
Aims and Objectives	**14**
Aims	14
Objectives	15
Structure and Content	**16**
Structure	16
Content	17
Collecting material	**19**
Copyright	**20**
Scripting the Presentation	**21**

3

PowerPoint 23

Creating a presentation	**23**
Saving your presentation	**25**
The PowerPoint window	**26**
The low-tech approach	**30**
Stand-alone	**30**

4

Alternative software 31

What's available	**31**
Word processor	31
WordArt	33
Textual Effects	34
Animated Text	35
Presentation applications	**36**
Presenter	36
Impress	38

5

A new presentation — 39

Template — 39
Ready Made Template — 40
Wizard — 43
Do it yourself — 48
Running order — 52
Linking slides — 54
   Adding a button — 55
   Action — 56
Automatic control — 57
   Timing — 57
Automatic presentation — 59
Notes — 59

6

What can be included… — 61

6a

Text — 63

Words and phrases — 63
   Entering text — 63
   Text style — 64
   Adding a text box — 65
   Text box effects — 65
Text tips — 70

6b

Photographs · 71

Digital camera	71
Scanning a photograph	72
Capturing from the web	72
Preparing pictures	**73**
Cropping a picture	73
Improving a photograph	75
Adding a border	76
Inserting pictures	**77**
Backgrounds	**79**

6c

Drawings · 81

Drawing control	**82**
Grid	83
Group	83
Align and Distribute	84
Objects	**85**
Lines	85
Shapes	88
Examples	**90**

6d

Animations · 91

File types	**91**
Creating animations	**92**
Highlights	92

Rotation	95
Saving	**96**
Placing the animation	**97**
Controlling the animation	98
Creating large animations	**100**
The first frame	101
Points to consider	**104**

6e

Video 105

How to capture	**105**
Placing a video clip	**109**
Controlling a video clip	110
Special effects	112

6f

Sound 113

Pre-recorded sound file	113
Controlling the sound	114
Recording a sound file	**116**
Direct recording	**119**
Playing a CD	**120**
Points to consider	**122**

6g

Charts and graphs 123

Types of graph	**123**
Creating a graph	**123**
Choosing the graph type	**125**
Graph titles	126
Layout styles	127

Finishing the chart	131
Cut and Paste	**132**
Organisation charts	**133**

6h

Other files and effects — 137

Drawing	**137**
Creating a drawing	137
Importing the file	140
Hyperlinks	**140**
Launching applications	**144**
Live camera (Action Settings)	144
MP3 Player (Insert Object)	146
Organisational Charts	**147**

7

Special effects — 149

Slide changes	**149**
Speed	150
Sound	150
Slide effects	**151**
Animation buttons	151
Effects buttons	152
Order of events	**153**
Custom animation	**154**
Animation order	**155**
Timing	155
Effects	156
Chart effect	156
Play settings	158
Setting your choices	**158**
When should I use them?	159

In the classroom	160
Stand alone	160

8

Display options — 161

Computer output	**161**
Large screen CRT monitors	163
Data projector	164
LCD Panel	166
Back projection	167
Pointing	167
Infrared presentation aid	168
Infrared keyboard	169
Interactive whiteboard	170
Large mouse pointer	**171**

9

Final preparation — 173

Almost ready	**173**
Speaker's notes	**173**
Rehearsal	**176**
Timing	176
Handouts for the audience	**177**
Questions	**179**
What should you take?	**180**
Introduction	**181**

10

Giving the presentation — 183

The big day	**183**
Setting up	183

Final rehearsal	186
The audience arrives	**186**
Introduction	186
You're on	**187**
Your first words…	**188**
Humour	188
Enthusiasm	188
Restraint	188
Confidence	189
Your stance	189
Involve the audience	189
Speaking	189
Questions	**190**
Coming to the end	**191**
Feedback	**192**

11

Pitfalls 193

12

Quick check 197

13

Software and hardware 201

Useful software addresses	**201**
Useful hardware addresses	**203**

14

Index 205

1

Introduction

Anyone who has attended talks, seminars or lessons which are illustrated using slides, overhead projector transparencies or computer generated presentations will know that they usually fall into one of two categories: good and bad. When they're good, they're very good, but when they're bad they're positively awful. This book focuses on the good practice.

Off the wall

People who have given talks, lectures or lessons will recognise the advantages of using pictures and charts to illustrate the key points of their talk. One picture can be worth a thousand words. I suppose the first people to realise this were our pre-historic ancestors who used the walls of their caves to draw and communicate their ideas and thoughts.

Centuries later, the blackboard was a common sight in classrooms all over the world. Curiously, the blackboard offered few advantages over most other flat, vertical surfaces including the inside of a cave. Apart from being easily cleaned, there was not much to recommend it. Even using so-called dust-free chalk, using a blackboard was a messy business. Long term use of sticks of chalk caused the skin to become dry as the chalk tended to absorb the natural skin oils, clothes became covered with dust and so every pre 1970's teacher looked like they had severe dandruff.

Nevertheless, the blackboard was widely used as it provided teachers with the only means of conveying notes and drawings to a whole class. Personally, I was never a fan. From the teacher's point of view, it was difficult to show some things on a blackboard, and your back was always facing the class whilst you wrote or drew. From a pupil's point of view, I can remember sitting in a class whilst the teacher wrote board-

1   Introduction

full after board-full of notes which we were expected to copy. If ever there was a scheme to put pupils to sleep, this was it.

Black to white

When I started teaching in the mid 1970's, whiteboards were becoming available. These were intended as a direct replacement for the dusty blackboard. They were certainly cleaner than blackboards, but beyond that they didn't offer many significant advantages. Early versions required special pens which could be erased without liquids - hence dry-wipe whiteboards. Unfortunately visiting teachers didn't always recognise the need to use specific pens and began writing on the board with any fibre-tipped pen they happened to have with them at the time. As a result, many class-rooms equipped with whiteboards were also  equipped with bottles of washing up liquid, scouring powder, white spirit, acetone and a variety of solvents to try to clean the board.

Modern versions are much better, but you still have to turn your back on the class whilst you are using it.

Overhead projector

The problem with early overhead projectors, or OHPs as they became affectionately known, is that you needed a virtual blackout to be able to see what was projected onto the screen.

Introduction

Clear sheets called acetates are written on using a special fibre tipped pen and are placed onto the OHP and projected onto a screen. An OHP offers three distinct advantages...

- You face your audience whilst writing on it. (Teachers will need no explanation as to why this is a benefit.)
- You write on a flat horizontal surface which is more natural than trying to write on a board screwed to a wall.
- You write normal size and the projector enlarges it. Again, this is much more natural and consequently OHP jottings tend to be neater that those written on a whiteboard.

Other benefits include the facility of being able to store pre-prepared acetates for use and re-use at a later date and it was this feature that led to modern illustrated presentations. I used to have a folder full of carefully drawn acetates which I would pull out at any time to illustrate a particular lesson.

For the first time, complicated diagrams and charts could be completed in advance and brought into the arena to be shown to large numbers of people. A trick that was frequently used was placing a 'blind' over the display so that only a part could be seen. As the talk progressed, the blind was moved down thus revealing more of what was previously hidden. Typically this method was used to reveal a number of 'bulleted points', one at a time - a technique that would reappear in talks that were illustrated with computer generated notes.

1 Introduction

Enter the computer

Like so many other activities, the computer has now entered into the proceedings and suddenly the concept of an illustrated presentation takes on a new dimension. It didn't take long to recognise that for illustrated talks, lessons and presentations, the computer can not only do most things better than other methods, but it can actually do things not previously possible.

For the first time, you can give a talk that can be illustrated with pictures, sounds and animations without needing to use a variety of projectors, televisions and videos to achieve it. The only piece of equipment you need to control the whole presentation is a computer which is set up to send the screen output to a display large enough that everyone can see.

Where can it be used?

There are three main ways in which a computer-generated presentation can be used which may influence the way in which the presentation is constructed...

Accompany a talk or lecture. More and more people are being asked to give a talk to colleagues about issues directly related to their business. These talks may be to people from other institutions or companies, or it may be by a member of management as a method of disseminating information in a way that will be interesting and stimulating.

In the classroom, teachers will find that illustrated lessons can motivate pupils in a way that traditional teaching does not.

Like traditional lessons, the presentations are usually linear: you begin at the beginning and view each slide one after the other, rather like the pages of a book.

1 Introduction

The presentation shown on the previous page is from a talk I gave to network managers. The slide is reproduced with permission from SfE.

Stand-alone display. A free-standing, automatically running display can provide an informative greeting for visitors, without the need to have someone on hand to repeat the introduction over and over again. Wherever visitors are expected at irregular intervals, such as a school open evening, or whenever an exhibit needs to be explained, a presentation can provide the solution.

More and more companies are using presentations provided on CD ROM or as an Internet download as a means of communicating their products to potential customers.

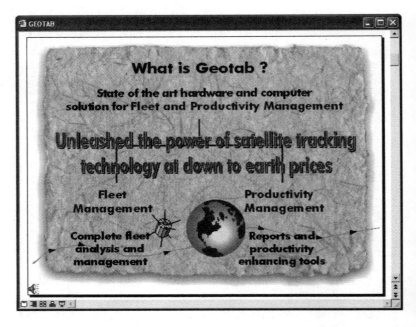

The example shown here is used with permission from GeoTab. Potential customers can download this presentation from the Internet

Introduction 1

and learn all about the product from the comfort of their own home. The presentation is completely self-contained and requires no human intervention: once the presentation is opened, it plays by itself.

Interactive learning module. This is a learning tool in which the user controls the presentation so that they can work at their own pace. It need not be linear (in other words, it need not be a presentation which starts at the beginning and works through sequentially to the end) but can be rather like a 'spider' where the user can branch off in different directions according to their particular learning needs.

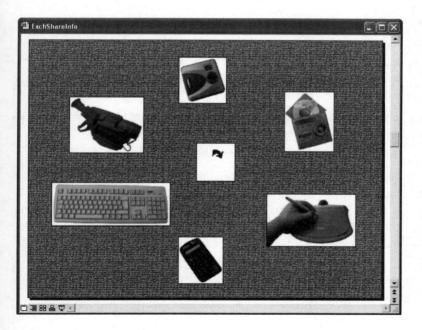

The slide shown here is from a presentation about multimedia and is intended for young children to research the subject themselves. Each of the pictures is a 'button' and when clicked on will open further information about the media.

1 Introduction

Although all three will be referred to either collectively or individually, the main focus of this book is the presentation to accompany a talk or lecture. When there is a particular difference between the different types, specific reference will be made to it.

Conventions used in this book

It is important to establish some conventions because there are words which can have more than one meaning.

Learning module. Or Interactive Learning Module or ILM. A computer based presentation in which an individual can work through the material in any order s/he chooses.

Presentation. (with a capital 'P'.) This refers to the whole talk, lesson, lecture or seminar, including the computer-generated element. Sometimes the Presentation is referred to as a talk or lecture to reduce the amount of repetition in the book.

presentation. (with a small 'p'.) This variation of the spelling refers to the computer element of the Presentation only.

Slide. One screen from your presentation.

Stand-alone. Sometimes you may be required to prepare a presentation which will not be used to accompany a talk. It will stand in a public place and run automatically in a never-ending loop. Some companies have even put their presentations onto the internet so would-be customers can learn about their products.

2

Planning

What first?

So, you've been asked to give a Presentation and you're expected to use a computer to illustrate your talk. The first thing to do is to congratulate yourself because somebody obviously thinks you have the ability and expertise to do it. The next thing to do is put your computer away, (unless you want to use it to take notes). You certainly won't need it to create your presentation yet.

Remember, the multimedia presentation is to illustrate your talk. It's not a good idea to attempt to create a presentation and then build your speech or lesson around it.

Planning applies equally to a stand-alone presentation: a little time spent at the outset could save a great deal of time later and without doubt will result in a much better presentation, whatever its purpose may be.

What type of presentation?

In this book we are looking at three distinct types of multimedia presentation. These are...

- to accompany a talk or lecture
- as a standalone display
- as an interactive learning module.

Although these three may appear to be quite different, they have, surprisingly, much in common. In particular, they all have an audience who will have specific requirements and expectations and a content which will address the issues you need/want to cover.

2 Planning

Who is your audience?

It is important to establish who you are going to be talking to, or in the case of a standalone presentation or interactive learning module, who will actually see it or use it. Clearly the answer is going to vary from one circumstance to another but you must bear in mind who you are aiming at so that you can pitch the content at the correct level.

If you aim too high, you will lose your audience. They won't understand what you are talking about and when you cast your eyes around the audience all you will see are glazed expressions. In the case of standalone or interactive learning modules, they simply won't be used.

If you aim too low, you'll put your audience to sleep through boredom. Some people may even be offended, and understandably so. How would you like it if you were dragged halfway across the country to hear someone speak about things you already know and which are obvious to anyone within your particular industry?

These points apply to interactive learning modules and standalone presentations, as well as presentations to accompany a talk, lesson or lecture.

The points you should consider are...

How many are coming? The number of people in the audience can have a dramatic effect on the way in which you give your presentation. A small number, i.e. 6, might mean that you could be sitting down at the same table with them. A group of over a 100 will certainly mean you'll be standing in front of them in a large hall.

Who will be there? The answer to this could also have a bearing on the way the presentation will be given. Will your audience largely comprise people who you know (i.e. work colleagues) or will they be mainly strangers? If the audience will contain anyone you won't know (or who won't know you) then you may need longer to build up a rapport with them.

Planning   2

Why will they be there? Are they coming because they want to, or have they been told that they must attend? Are they coming in what they perceive as their own time or are they in the firm's time? If they've been told they must attend, then they may be hostile towards you. If they've been told they must attend *and* it is in their own time then you can be fairly certain they don't want to be there and could do their best to ensure that you know the fact.

What will they know? Are they coming to hear about a subject on which they know nothing, or do they already have a degree of expertise in the field on which you will be talking? Clearly, the answer to this question will have a significant bearing on the content of your presentation. If they are professionals in the same field as you, then it's worth trying to find out what they are likely to know.

The Location

The venue can have a dramatic effect on how you deliver your Presentation and how successful it is. If possible, visit the venue before you give your Presentation so that you can get an idea of what it will be like to speak in that particular environment.

In many cases the venue may be known to you. You may have used it before. It may be an office or classroom in the same building in which you work, but however familiar you think you are with the location, unless you've actually given a presentation there before, visit it again.

More and more companies are using special venues in which to give Presentations. Try phoning the venue to ask them for details about the place where you will be speaking. They may be able to email or fax a plan of the lecture theatre. It's worth trying to learn as much about the location as possible: that knowledge will put you more at ease. At the very least, it's one less thing to worry about.

Further points you should consider about the location…

How do I get there? This is another obvious point, but amidst all the careful planning and preparation, it's easily overlooked. Find out exactly

2 Planning

where the venue is, how to get there and how long it will take to get there. If you're going by car, is there a car park or should you go by public transport?

Is it worth staying in a hotel? Very often the lecture theatres used by companies for corporate Presentations are part of a hotel. If they are, or there is a hotel nearby, consider staying there overnight. Knowing that all you have to do is climb out of bed and walk down a flight of stairs is great deal less stressful that having to catch a train to an unfamiliar destination, possibly having to change to another train, or bus or both. It's also a lot less stressful than trying to fight your way through rush hour traffic.

What type of venue is it? Is it a purpose-built lecture theatre, or a bare hall with stacking chairs that have to be set out first? How will the seating be arranged? Will you be expected to speak on a stage or a platform? Will you be able to move around as you talk or are you going to be tied to a lectern?

What are the audio qualities? If you're going to be expected to speak into a microphone and you've never used one before, see if there is any way you can get some practice first. If you are asked to use a microphone it will probably be because your voice, however powerful it may be, would not be easily heard in the venue due to its size or poor acoustic qualities. Check if the microphone will be on a stand or a clip-on type. If it's the latter, is it a wireless type or will you be dragging a lead around?

What visual aids are there? You will probably be using some electrical items (computer, OHP, etc). Are there enough sockets to plug everything in? If you are going to use some sort of projector (slide projector, data projector, etc) find out where it is relative to where you will be. If it's mounted at table height, beware of casting shadows on it. If it's ceiling mounted there is less likelihood of shadows.

Planning 2

About the Presentation

Your Presentation may be part of a larger event so you'll also need to understand a little about it. If you've been asked by someone to give the Presentation, you should find out from them as much as you can about their expectations.

How long? You'll need to know how long you will be expected to talk so that you can plan your Presentation accordingly. You'll need to refer to the time budget regularly as you work your way through preparing your Presentation.

When is the start? Not only should you know when you will be expected to start, but also when the meeting/conference commences.

How many speakers? You may be the only speaker, but you could be one of a number of speakers. You will need to know how many others and where in the running order your slot has been put. If you are one of several speakers, then the time factor becomes even more critical.

Who will they be? It's worth knowing who else will be speaking, but even more important is finding out what they will be saying. Are they, for example, going to be saying something which is in direct conflict with what you will be saying?

Will there be questions? If you know your subject, questions should not be a particular issue, although it is worth considering what questions are likely to be asked so you can prepare some answers. Generally if questions are allowed, there will be a session either at the end of each speaker's turn or at the end of the whole session. You should not get a stream of questions during your presentation unless you specifically want to. Teachers, for example, might choose to ask questions and permit questions and discussion during the Presentation. This would not normally be the case for business Presentations.

2 Planning

Is there a dress code? You will need to be comfortable, but you also need to dress according to the occasion. It is particularly important that you observe any dress code if you are one of several speakers. You will feel very uncomfortable if the other speakers are dressed in suits and you look as if you're en route to the beach. Similarly you don't want to be over-dressed. If in doubt, go for the middle ground. Men should wear a suit or a dark jacket and smart trousers, a light shirt with a tie. Choose the tie carefully: the safest is blue and red stripes but definitely not one covered in cartoon characters. Women are usually safest wearing a suit with either a skirt or trousers, and a light blouse.

Avoid an over-abundance of jewellery - the audience will not want to be distracted.

Aims and Objectives

Aims

It may seem obvious, but it is vital that you outline precisely what it is you think your presentation should give to your audience. You will need to carefully consider what the aim or aims of the Presentation are. In some cases this will be self-evident but it is important to spend time considering what the point of the Presentation actually is.

When asked to give a Presentation, the aim may be unclear – sometimes even to the person who has asked you! You have been asked because, presumably, you have a degree of expertise in this particular field, but are you being asked to introduce novices to the subject, or are you being asked to extend the knowledge of current experts by putting forward new or controversial theories? Clearly the two aims are about as far apart as it is possible to be, and unless the aim is established at the outset, you're going to be heading for difficulties.

You may need to ask the person who asked you to give the Presentation about their intended aims. If they don't know, which is not unknown, you will need to established the aims yourself, based on the

Planning 2

other information you have previously collected such as who the audience will be and why they are coming.

The aim should be able to be written in a single statement and outlines the goal you wish to achieve. The aim(s) would normally begin with the word 'To'...

- To outline the new learning strategy.
- To show owners how to care for their dog.
- To demonstrate the benefits of using our product.
- To show how salt can be extracted from brine.
- To show how to manage a computer network.

Objectives

The objectives are the steps that will need to be taken to achieve the aims. Taking the first example, *To outline the new learning strategy*, the objectives might be...

- Why there is a need for a new strategy.
- How the strategy is expected to improve attainment.
- How the strategy builds on previous good practice.
- How to manage the strategy.

There may also be some issues that you would prefer to hide. These are sometimes called negative objectives...

- The additional preparation required.
- Evening training sessions.

2 Planning

You may also have some personal objectives...

> - Demonstrate to the Management that I am fully conversant with my subject.
> - Show that I am a confident and competent speaker.

Like the aims, it pays to get the objectives clearly established before proceeding any further. Without them is going to be like walking in the dark, not knowing where you're going and not even knowing where you *want* to go.

Structure and Content

Structure

It is vital to structure your presentation carefully in order to...

- maintain interest
- aid understanding
- ensure all points are covered.

It's easy to spot a Presentation that hasn't been carefully structured. They are often difficult to follow because they jump around between different points and it's difficult to maintain interest because you can't follow any particular train of thought. From the audience's standpoint, reflecting on an unstructured Presentation is often difficult because you can't tie your thoughts to any clear progression of ideas.

In short, you will probably fail to achieve some or many of the aims and objectives you previously outlined.

Planning 2

When working out a suitable structure, in general, it's best to start with a clear beginning, have a well-defined middle and finally an end.

There is an old maxim that is equally applicable today as it was with pre-computerised presentations:

- Tell them what you're going to tell them.
- Tell them
- Tell them what you've told them.

In other words, use your introduction to outline what you are going to cover in the Presentation. After that will be the main part of the Presentation where you will convey the message, teach the module, etc. Finally, for your conclusion, sum up what you've said.

Content

You are now at the stage of considering how you are going to deliver each objective. When you are outlining the content, not only should you list the points that are to be covered, but you may also want to consider some points which do not need to be covered: points that you can reasonably assume they already know. For example, it may be that this particular Presentation builds on a previous lesson so you'll need to refer back to who your audience is and what they are likely to already know. This process will help you pitch your presentation at the correct level.

Deciding what you want the audience to learn may require some research in order to ensure all relevant points are covered and that you've got your facts straight. You may have a syllabus to work to or you may have some reference material from which you may extract some points that you may not have previously considered.

It may be helpful to use your computer's word processor to list the points. Begin by writing a list of points that you want to address.

In the case of the presentation about Labradors (referred to on page 77), which was created for a school project and is used with Sally

2 Planning

Preston's permission, the list of points that she wanted to cover looks rather like a table of contents…

> - Background
> - Chips
> - Exercise
> - Healthy Food
> - Pet Passports
> - Treats
> - Bedtime
> - Collars and leads
> - Grooming
> - Identification
> - Toys
> - Vaccinations

These points are not in any particular order and so you may want to rearrange them so that one follows on logically from another. As you begin putting your Presentation together, you may think of one or two points you want to add. It's usually fairly easy to insert new sections in the middle of your Presentation, but trying to add lots of new points can make the Presentation look (and feel) rather haphazard.

Each point that you want to cover should be given some detail so that you know exactly what needs to be to covered in each point. Continuing the example of the Labrador project…

> **Chips:** What is a chip?
> How do chips work?
> How are they applied?
> Why chip your dog?
> Types of chip?
> The Law relating to stray dogs.
> Things that can go wrong.

Planning 2

Each point should be clearly outlined so that you are in no doubt that you have included everything you need to and you know what you are to prepare.

Collecting material

It is possible, and even probable, that much of the material you will need is readily available to you. After all, if you have been asked to give the Presentation because you're an expert, it is likely that you'll have a great deal of information about the subject stored in your head. What you may need to collect are pictures, tables and charts to illustrate your Presentation.

If you are not an expert, you may need to research the subject and find a source for materials. The subject on which you are giving the Presentation will possibly determine where the best place to get materials will be. For most subjects, a good place to start is the Internet. It may be that you know of a specific site. Your company may have such a site, so might one of its competitors.

If you're not sure, a simple search can be carried out by just typing a keyword into the address bar of the browser...

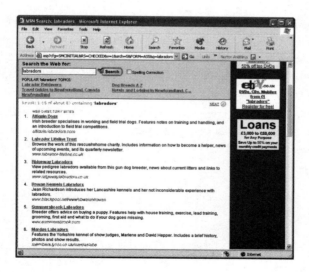

2   Planning

Entering the word 'labradors' generates an index of over 80 articles. Some articles will not be of any use as they may be about a totally different subject like the Labrador Brewing Company that brews specialist beers and ales.

Clicking on one of the links will take you to that site where you will (hopefully) find information and material that will be of use to you.

Be aware that Internet sites do not necessarily contain factually accurate information so it's worth cross checking with similar material on other sites.

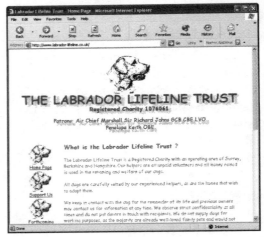

Copyright

It is essential you get permission to use any material you find in books, magazines, newspapers and Internet articles. This refers to pictures as well as any written material. For Presentations there is usually no problem: it's when you want to print the material in a book that people begin looking more closely at copyright.

If nothing else, it is courteous to ask first and you should refer to sources of any material either as a credit accompanying a picture or passage, or at the end of the Presentation.

Planning 2

Scripting the Presentation

At this point you should have...

- a clear idea of the content of your Presentation
- gathered and verified all the information required
- a clear idea of the order.

As you were preparing your aims, objectives, structure and content you will probably have started to formulate some ideas about what you are going to say and how you are going to say it. Now is the time to put those thoughts down on paper and prepare what you are going to say.

You can deliver your Presentation in one of three ways. You can either...

- ad-lib
- prepare a speech which you read out
- prepare notes to guide you through the content.

Only *you* can decide which is going to suit you best, but you may wish to consider the following...

To ad-lib your way through a 30 - 60 minute Presentation takes skill and nerve in equally large quantities. You need to be very confident that you are fully conversant with every aspect of your subject to the point where you can talk about it in your sleep. Although the audience could get a smoother, more flowing performance, the main problems with ad-libbing are...

- losing your train of thought
- getting 'tongue-tied'
- forgetting to mention something of importance.

2 Planning

The safest way is to prepare a word-for-word script that you read out. The problem with that method is…

- your notes will be long and there is a danger you will lose your place
- unless you are really skilled, it will sound like what it is: a script being read out
- as a result of the last point, you may not come across as being confident in what you're saying.

A better way is to list a number of 'signposts' to guide you through what you are going to say. You can write these on postcards as brief headings or key words, or use as a guide the presentation you are going to show to accompany your talk.

The advantage with this method is that…

- you won't have to read through a thick pile of papers with notes
- which means there will be less danger of you 'getting lost'
- as you have a guide you won't miss anything
- you can adjust the speed of your delivery to fit into the time frame.

Whatever method you choose, you will almost certainly have to begin by putting down a few notes which you may either use to prompt you during your talk, expand into a full speech or memorise if you are going to speak without any prompts.

In addition, the notes could form the basis of a multimedia presentation to accompany your talk.

3
PowerPoint

It is now almost obligatory to use some sort of visual aid to accompany a Presentation. The visual element may be slides on an overhead projector, 35mm photo slides or a computer-generated presentation. There are several purpose-made computer applications designed to create presentations, but the best known seems to be Microsoft's PowerPoint. So well-known and widespread is this application that computer assisted talks have actually become known as 'PowerPoint Presentations', even if MS PowerPoint isn't actually being used.

As PowerPoint is the most widely known and used, it is this application that will be used throughout this book, although there are others which offer similar features and which operate in a similar way.

Creating a presentation

When PowerPoint is started a dialog opens which gives you the choice of creating a document using the wizard (which takes you step by step through the process of creating a presentation), using one of the pre-defined templates (which provides a sort of corporate identity to your presentation), or by creating a blank presentation.

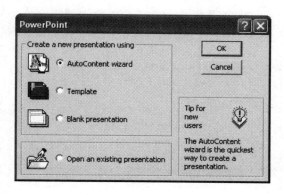

3   PowerPoint

To begin with, to get you used to the way PowerPoint works, click the radio button alongside **Blank presentation** and click the **OK** button. This opens a second dialog from which you may select the layout that most suits the first slide you want to create.

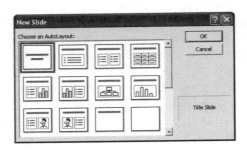

The first page will probably be the title page, so click once on the top left page layout icon and click the **OK** button to create a new PowerPoint document which will eventually become a presentation. The default size of the slide is in the ratio of 4:3 which is the exact aspect ratio of a computer monitor. In other words, unlike a word processor, PowerPoint creates a file that fits the monitor and not a particular size of paper.

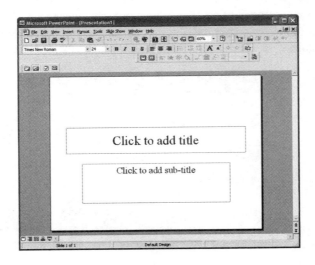

PowerPoint 3

Saving your presentation

At this stage it's a good idea to save your work. Click on the disc icon on the button bar at the top of the window which will open a standard file window. Enter the name of your presentation in the panel at the bottom and click the **Save** button.

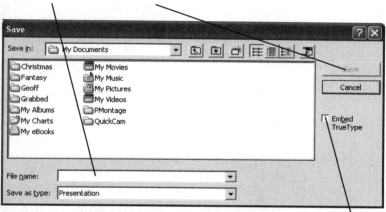

On the right is a button that doesn't appear in many applications: **Embed TrueType**. This is for presentations that will be run on a different computer to that which was used to create it. If, in its creation, you used some fancy fonts or font symbols, then ticking this option will ensure that your presentation will display correctly even if the computer you are running the presentation on does not have the correct fonts installed in it.

If in any doubt, click this option, but be aware that the resulting file will occupy significantly more disc space than the same file without embedded fonts. This is because the file will now have at least one complete set of font definitions embedded in it. Even if you use just 1 character from one font type, the whole font file will be included when the presentation is saved.

If transporting your presentation is a problem because you don't have the means to move large files, then you may have no choice other than to stick to one common font (e.g. Times New Roman or Arial, which

3 PowerPoint

everyone has) and untick the **Embed TrueType** box when you save. Check with the owner of the computer on which you intend to give your presentation that the fonts used in your presentation have been installed.

Organisations who contract speakers to prepare Presentations for them, often supply their own font or fonts which you should use when preparing your presentation.

Loading your presentation

To reload your presentation, double click on it and it will launch the PowerPoint application ready for you to continue editing it.

The PowerPoint window

The window in which PowerPoint operates is not dissimilar to that of a word processor. Many of the features are the same, but there are a couple of unusual extras.

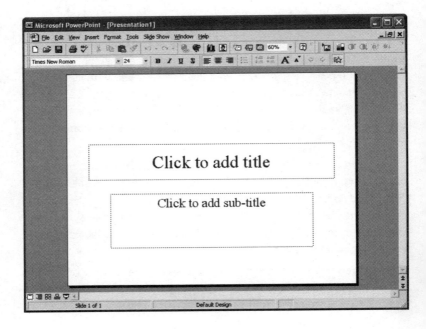

The font styles have inherited an extra button. This
is Shadowed text and, as the name clearly states,
it adds a light grey shadow behind the text giving

the impression that the text has been raised off the surface of the page.

The large and small letters will increase or decrease the font size by 4 points. This is a quick and convenient method of adjusting font size to fit a fairly limited space.

Both of these features work best when the text you want to alter is marked (either double click on a word or click and drag the mouse over a phrase). With the text marked, adjust the font size and/or apply an effect like Bold or Shadow.

The star icon opens a menu for adding a variety of animated effects like text moving onto the slide from the edge. When this button is clicked on, an additional row of buttons opens providing you with some simple effects which can be applied to either the title or to other textual elements of a particular slide. Once again, it's usually best to mark the element you want to add an animation to.

At the bottom left of the screen are five icons that determine how PowerPoint displays the presentation.

The left icon is the standard **Slide View** as shown opposite and it is in this view that most of the layout will be done. Although you can add text and adjust the size in some other views, in the slide view you will be able to move elements around the slide.

To view other slides in the presentation, drag the scroll bar on the right-hand side, or click once in the space either side of the scroll bar to jump up or down one slide.

Icon number two is the **Outline View** and shows the contents from each slide in a list, with a thumbnail of the currently selected slide on the right.

3   PowerPoint

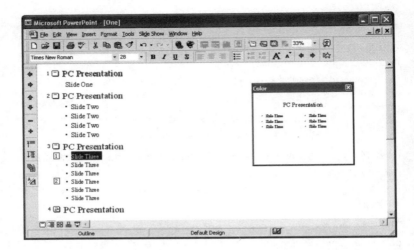

You may edit any of the text shown on the left and alterations will appear on the slide.

The centre icon is the **Sort View** and in this format you can easily sort the slides into a different order.

The last but one icon is the **Notes Page View** and shows a text box beneath the slide in which you can use, optionally to add notes for your talk.

Finally, the icon on the extreme right of the group of five is the **Slide Show View** and selecting this will fill the screen with the slide, with no window borders or tools. Normally slide number one will be the first slide to be seen, but as we will see later, this need not necessarily be the case.

In this mode…

- clicking the left mouse button
- pressing space
- pressing return
- pressing the right arrow key

… will advance the presentation by one slide.

PowerPoint 3

Pressing...

- the left arrow key
- backspace

... will return to the previous slide.

Escape will end the slide show and PowerPoint will revert to the last view.

Whilst in the **Slide Show View**, clicking the right-hand mouse button will open a menu which includes options to move forward or back and to exit the slide show.

Further options include hiding the mouse pointer (which will remain hidden until the mouse is moved) and changing the mouse pointer for a pen which will enable you to 'draw' on the slide in a pen colour of your choice.

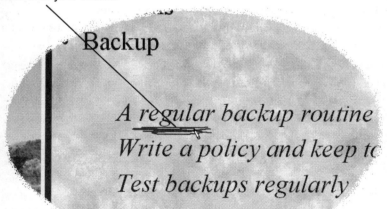

If you're going to use this feature, then a graphics tablet and pen is a better proposition than a mouse as you will be able to draw more naturally. This is explained in more detail on page 167.

29

3 PowerPoint

Lo-tech approach

The default PowerPoint slide size fits the 4:3 screen used by most computers, but you can change this size so that you can print out the slides onto acetate sheets that can be used on an overhead projector.

Go to the **File** menu and choose **Page Setup...** to open a dialog.

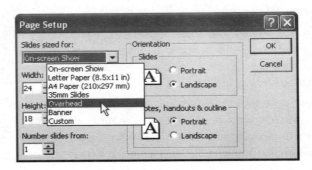

Click on the downward pointing arrow and choose the medium you intend using from the list. If you prefer, you may choose a custom size and enter your own page dimensions.

Most inkjet printers can print onto acetate sheets although you may need to buy a special ink cartridge for acetate.

Stand-alone

To ensure that PowerPoint presentations can be read by anyone and everyone, there is a special free version of PowerPoint. This version cannot be used to create PowerPoint presentations, but can read them. When taking your presentation to another location it is worth taking along the read-only version so that if PowerPoint isn't available for whatever reason, you can still run your presentation.

This file is available from Microsoft's website at www.microsoft.com. When you arrive at the site, enter 'PowerPoint' in the search tool.

4
Alternative software

What's available

Although this book focuses mainly on PowerPoint, there are several alternatives. There are other purpose-designed presentation applications and these will probably be the best choice. But even if you don't have one of these specialist programs, you can still create a very respectable presentation with other applications that may not have been specifically designed with this purpose in mind.

Word processor

Yes, even the humble word processor, which surely everyone will have, can be used to create some very acceptable presentations. If you have Windows running on your computer then you will have WordPad which is supplied with all versions of Windows. It will enable you to include some of the features normally found in a presentation, including pictures and bulleted points.

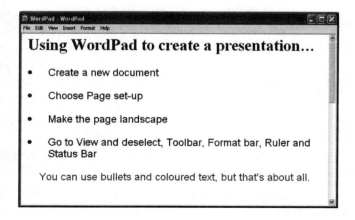

4   Alternative software

The problem with using a word processor is one of control. Not many word processors allow you to switch from one page to the next without using the mouse to scroll down. When using a word processor as a word processor, this is not a problem. Where you're standing up giving a talk and trying to concentrate on what you're saying, it's not always easy to carry out a fairly delicate operation with the mouse.

If you feel that a word processor will be suitable for your presentation, then you might consider using Microsoft's Word which has many more features than WordPad.

Word will allow you to do a great deal more than just display text. There are several effects that can be use to enhance each of the pages or slides.

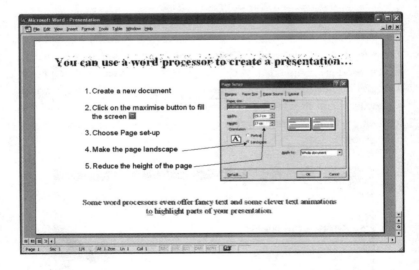

As you can see from the picture above, not only can pictures be included but they can be finely positioned which gives a better chance of creating a balanced slide. There is also a limited drawing facility enabling you to include arrows.

Word offers several interesting features which you may find useful when preparing a presentation.

Alternative software 4

WordArt. If you want to make your heading stand out, try using WordArt. Click on the ◂ icon to open the WordArt dialog and choose a style and click **OK**.

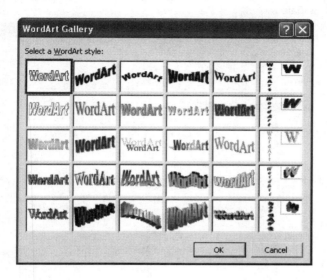

Then, enter the title in the box provided. You can also choose the font style and size from this dialog.

When the title has been placed on the screen you can centre it using the text alignment buttons and you can scale the text by dragging one of the nodes (the white squares) at the corners. The yellow diamond at the bottom allows you to shear the word - by dragging to the left you will slant the text to the right.

4   Alternative software

Textual effects. Apart from bullets (in a variety of styles) and numbers, you can highlight text in some interesting ways. Select a piece of text you want to apply an effect to, open the **Format** menu and choose **Font** to open a dialog.

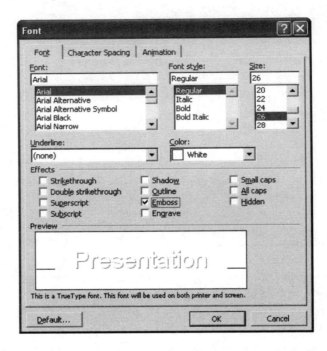

In the centre of the area marked **Effects**, are four textual effects that may prove useful for titles and headings. The preview at the bottom of the dialog shows what the text would look like.

Alternative software 4

Animated text. MS Word also includes the option of highlighting a piece of text with a simple animation. The variations include stars floating around the text, and text which shimmers. To apply one of these to a heading or caption, open the **Font** dialog as previously described and click the **Animation** tab.

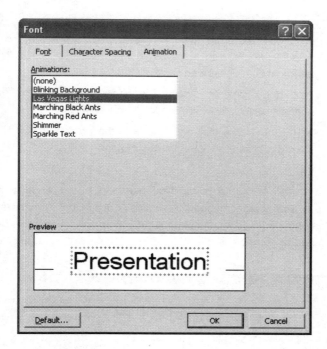

Choose the animation effect from the list. Again, the preview window shows you what you'll get.

There are several other tricks available in some of the more advanced word processors including coloured text and coloured backgrounds to add impact to your presentation. Bulleted and numbered text is also available in many word processors, including Word. Some even allow you to define the bullet style.

4   Alternative software

Presentation applications

Although it is possible to create a presentation with software that was not specifically designed for the job, there is little doubt that a purpose-designed presentation tool is far better for three reasons...

1. Moving between slides can be done with a simple key press. You don't have to fiddle with a mouse to position the slide exactly where you want it. It can even be made to run automatically if required.
2. You don't have to display the borders, frames and control buttons associated with Windows applications.
3. All the tools are included to create the presentation including (in most cases) clever animated effects.

Presenter. This program is by Textease and has a huge array of features including pre-designed templates. Each template has its own colour scheme with text pre-set at a particular size. You can use the template as is, or modify it to suit the presentation you intend to give.

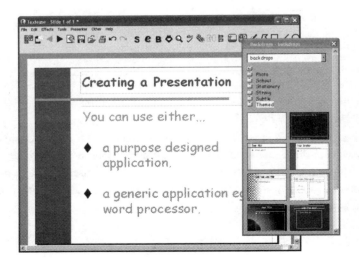

Alternative software 4

Presenter also includes a features which makes it especially suitable for children to use: built-in speech synthesis. It is easy to set up your presentation so that the text can be automatically narrated by the computer. It is unlikely you would want to use this feature in a presentation to accompany a talk, but for individual learning modules it means that users who do not have a firm grasp of English can still follow the text.

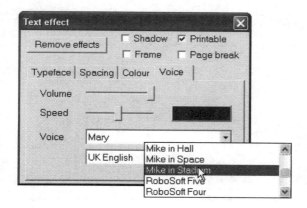

There are several voices to choose from and you can even make the text highlight itself as it's being read by the computer.

When the program opens, you begin by choosing a template. Additional slides can be added to the presentation which need not be identical copies of the first slide, but can be based on the same theme.

To ensure you will be able to run your finished Presenter presentation, there is a freely downloadable read-only version of the application on the Textease website (www.textease.com/). Once you've downloaded the application (called Browser), it can be freely copied and distributed. You cannot create presentations with it, merely read them. Alternatively, you can save your presentation as an HTML file and read it through a web browser such as Internet Explorer or Netscape Navigator.

4   Alternative software

Impress. This application is part of the Star Office suite and can be freely downloaded from the Sun website (www.sun.com/staroffice/) or purchased on CD ROM in which case you simply pay for the media (ie the disc itself), the manual and the packaging.

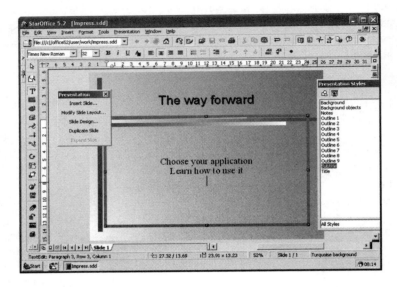

This application includes dozens of templates and some special effects to jazz up your presentation.

When the application is started you are presented with a wizard called AutoPilot which takes you through the stages of styling your presentation.

The five steps enable you to quickly choose the style, layout and font characteristics as well as the special effects which include fades between slides. If you want the presentation to run automatically, you can set the length of time the page is displayed.

5

A new presentation

Having decided the running order, and with your notes more or less sorted, you can begin creating the actual presentation.

Template

Like the pages of a book, in most cases the slides in the same presentation should have a degree of uniformity. If you have been asked to give a Presentation you may be provided with a template on which to create your presentation. SfE, for example, provide this stylish template which ensures that not only every slide in a presentation will be consistent, but every Presentation given for the company will have a corporate appearance.

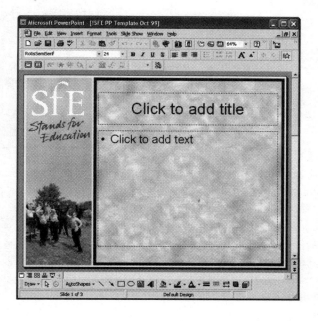

5 A new presentation

If you have not been provided with a template, then you should begin by creating one and PowerPoint provides three ways of doing this.

1.. Ready-made template

If the full version of PowerPoint has been installed in your computer you will have access to a number of templates which are ready to use. Click on the **Start** button and select **New Office Document** from the menu to open the **New Office Document** dialog. One of the tabs at the top of the dialog will be headed **Presentation Designs** and clicking this will display all the templates currently available.

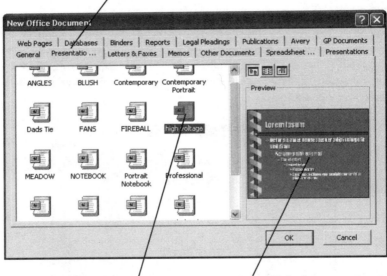

In most cases, clicking once on one of the files will display a preview in the right area of the dialog. Some of the designs will not be to your personal taste but you should find something that is acceptable.

Using one of the ready-made templates you will be able to create a presentation very quickly and which will impress everyone. Unless, that is, there is someone in your audience who also uses this particular presentation creation tool and will immediately recognise exactly what you've done.

A new presentation   5

But you can go some way towards disguising the template. When you have selected the design, you will be asked to choose the layout of the first page. This is discussed in more detail later, for the moment, choose the layout on the top left and click **OK**.

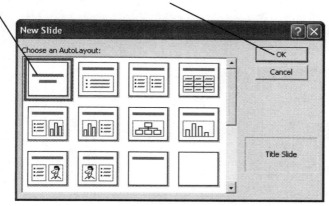

You will then see the page on the screen. Go to the **Format** menu and choose **Slide Color Scheme...** which will open the following dialog.

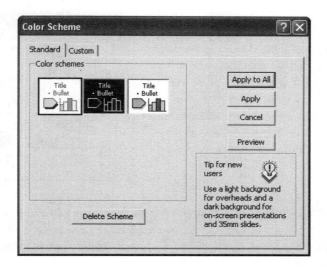

5 A new presentation

The tip on the right side is worth noting: use a light background if you are going to be printing the slides onto transparent film and showing them on an overhead projector. If you are intending to show the slides on a computer, use a darker background.

Click on the **Custom** tab and you will be given the opportunity to alter individual colours on either a single slide or every slide in the presentation.

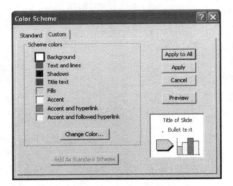

Click on one of the elements of the design from the list on the left and click the **Change Color...** button.

This opens another dialog from where you can pick an alternative colour from the chart. In the unlikely event that the colour you want is not shown in the hexagonal colour chart, you can click the **Custom** tab which will display a greater number of colours.

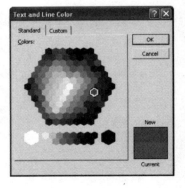

Click **OK** to close the last dialog and then click the **Apply to All** button if you want the alterations to be applied to every slide in your presentation, or the **Apply** button if you just want it applied to the slide you are currently displaying.

A new presentation   **5**

2.. Wizard

The AutoContent Wizard provided with PowerPoint is a clever way of getting a presentation together very quickly. It takes you though a series of simple steps which results in a complete presentation with all of the important elements in place. Once you've gone through the wizard, all you have to do is add the text and any pictures and diagrams you want to include. All the design and layout have been done for you.

The drawback with this method is that, like the use of the ready-made templates, you end up with a rather impersonal presentation.

Click on the **Start** button and select **New Office Document** from the menu to open the **New Office Document** dialog. One of the tabs at the top of the dialog will be headed **Presentations**.

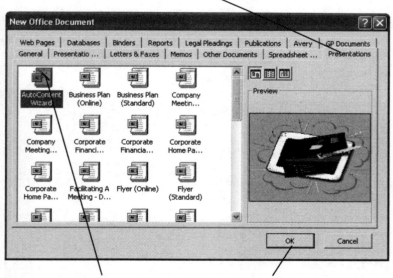

Select the **AutoContent Wizard** and click the **OK** button to start the wizard.

43

5 A new presentation

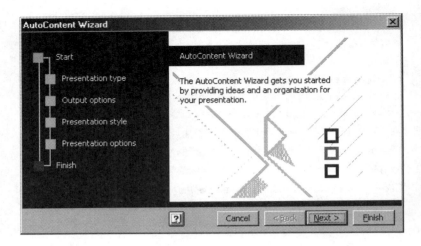

The first screen simply introduces the concept of using a wizard. Clicking on the **?** button will provide help. At any time you can click **Finish** or **Cancel**, but in most cases click the **Next** button to take you on to the next stage.

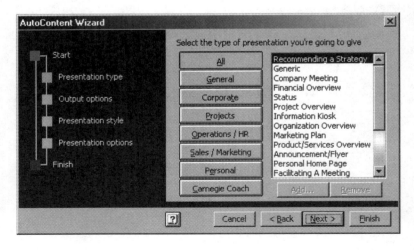

Here you choose the presentation type from either **All** available or from one of the categories.

A new presentation

After choosing the presentation, clicking **Next** takes you on to deciding how your presentation will be used.

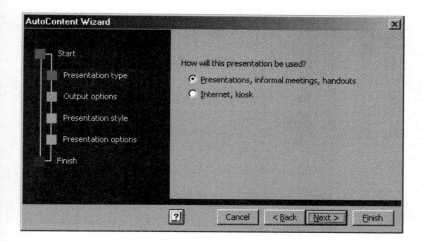

Your choice will determine some of the characteristics of the layout and will be the one best suited to the medium you intend using. Clicking **Next** takes you to a similar dialog asking you to choose how the presentation will be output.

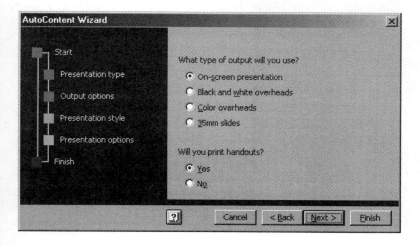

5 A new presentation

The last but one dialog invites you to enter details about the presentation and about yourself.

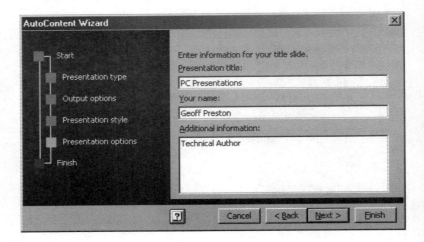

Finally, clicking **Next** takes you to the last dialog in the wizard.

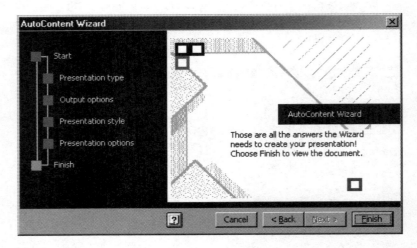

You may go back and change any of your selections or click the **Finish** button.

A new presentation 5

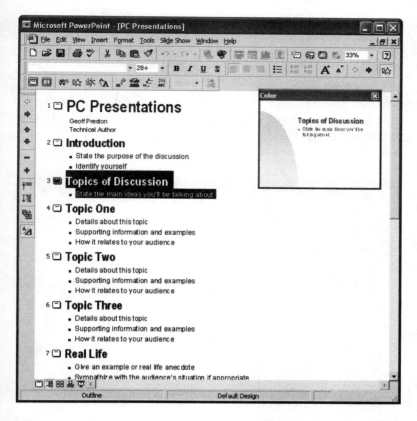

What you end up with is a complete presentation comprising a dozen or so slides, each with a consistent appearance. Colours, title characteristics and text size will have been determined, as well as a running order.

When the presentation is first displayed, it is shown in its outline format. Clicking on one of the screen icons alongside the slide number will display a thumbnail of the screen as it will currently appear. The text can be edited either in the outline format or if you prefer, by changing to the slide format by clicking on the left-hand icon at the bottom of the PowerPoint window. You can alter any of the characteristics, including changing the running order. This is explained later.

5　A new presentation

3.. Do it yourself

This is not as tricky as one might at first imagine as there are lots of elements provided in PowerPoint that you can easily apply to your design.

Begin by opening PowerPoint. Go to the **File** menu and choose **New...** to open a new document. This will open a dialog from which you must choose a layout. This will be explained in more detail later, but for the moment choose the layout at the top left of the dialog and click **OK**.

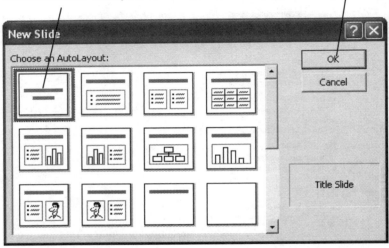

This will open a blank page with text frames in which you can add a title and put some additional description.

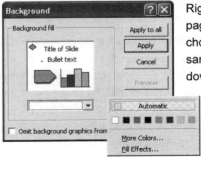

Right-click on a blank area of the page to open a context menu and choose **Background...** . Under the sample on the left of the dialog is a downward facing arrow alongside a rectangle. The rectangle contains the current background colour and usually begins as white. Click on the arrow to

A new presentation 5

open a menu from which you may choose a new colour for the background. At the bottom of the menu is **Fill Effects...** and selecting this option leads to a dialog offering numerous background effects.

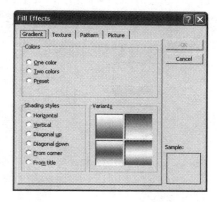

You may place a graduated fill, a texture, a pattern or a picture in the background. **Gradient** and **Pattern** have several options, relating to colour and direction. Clicking the **Texture** tab offers the user the opportunity to place one of about a dozen pictures in the background representing textures such as marble, stone, hessian and wood.

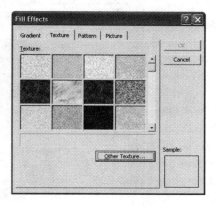

When you have chosen a suitable texture, click **OK**.

49

5 A new presentation

The last option is **Picture** and if you choose to place a photograph in the background, you'll need to choose the subject very carefully, or be prepared to do some careful cropping. Click on the **Select Picture...** button and a dialog will open which will enable you to navigate around your computer to locate the picture you require.

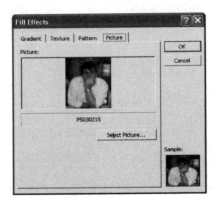

Regardless of the size of the picture you choose, it will be stretched to fill the slide. This will inevitably cause a degree of distortion, but will be most noticeable when the picture chosen is portrait (the longest side vertical) as it will make the subject look rather squashed. Sometimes this can barely be seen, but pictures which include a face look obviously wrong.

The section on photographs on page 79 details how pictures may be prepared for backgrounds.

A new presentation

When you have chosen your background, clicking the **Apply** button will place the background on the current slide only. Clicking **Apply to All** will place it on every slide.

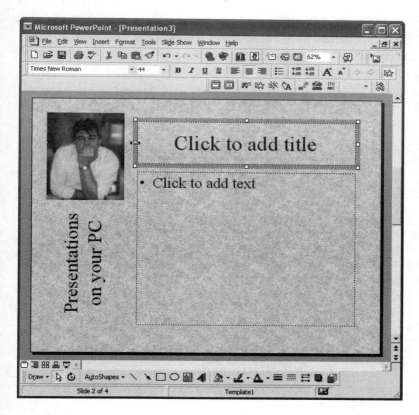

The text frames can, if necessary, be resized so that they fit with your background. This is achieved by clicking on the dotted line that marks the frame position. Eight square markers will appear around the frame and these can be dragged into position to re-size and/or re-position the frame.

At any stage, you can replace phrases like 'Click to add text' with the text of your presentation.

5   A new presentation

Running order

At this stage you should know approximately how many slides will need to be created and what will be on each slide. The next stage is the get all of the slides in place.

If you used one of the ready-made templates or you have a custom template either supplied for you or one you created yourself, you will need to add the slides you require for the presentation.

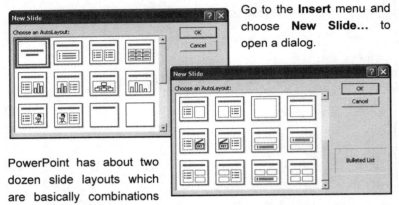

Go to the **Insert** menu and choose **New Slide...** to open a dialog.

PowerPoint has about two dozen slide layouts which are basically combinations of text boxes and/or spaces for a graphic which will be placed over your chosen background.

To add a new slide, click on the design you want and then click **OK**. The slide will be placed immediately after the one currently displayed.

If you used the wizard then you will have a file with about a dozen slides already in place. Slides can be deleted by going to the **Edit** menu and choosing **Delete Slide**.

Once a new slide has been inserted into your presentation you can make adjustments to the frames in the way previously described on the previous page.

A new presentation 5

Slides can also be rearranged by clicking on the centre icon at the bottom left of the PowerPoint window.

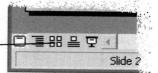

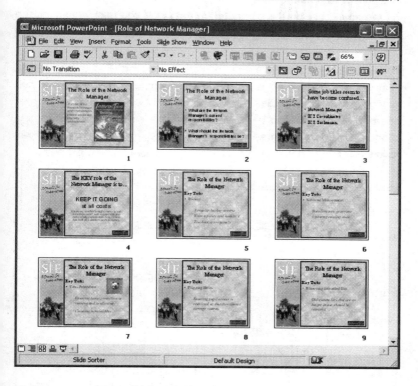

Moving one or more slides can alter the running order of a presentation. Click on the slide you wish to move and drag it between two other slides. This simple process enables you to completely rearrange your entire presentation, although it has to be said that if it had been thoroughly planned, it shouldn't be necessary to do a great deal of rearranging.

5   A new presentation

Linking slides

So far all we have looked at are linear presentations. In other words, like a book, you begin at the beginning and view each slide in turn until you reach the end. For presentations that accompany a talk or a lecture, this is the best way as all the speaker has to do to move between slides is hit the space bar on the computer keyboard. If you accidentally hit the space bar twice then pressing the key with the left facing arrow will take you back one slide.

In some circumstances, further control is required. For example, you may want to create a 'learning module' whereby the end user can navigate around the slides depending on what s/he wishes to learn. A linear presentation can be represented by a straight line: a learning module is rather like a tree where the user begins at the base and can follow any one of a number of branches to achieve a particular goal.

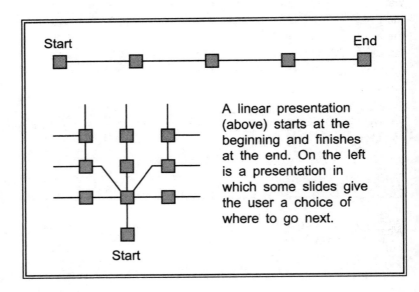

A linear presentation (above) starts at the beginning and finishes at the end. On the left is a presentation in which some slides give the user a choice of where to go next.

A new presentation 5

Linking slides in a fashion other than linear requires the addition of two things...

- a button to click with the mouse
- a destination slide

Adding a button

Display the slide on which you intend placing the button, go to the **Slide Show** menu and move down to **Action Buttons** to open a menu showing a dozen button types.

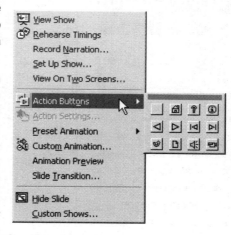

The only difference between the buttons is the legend on them. Choose the one you want by clicking on it and the button will be placed on the slide. There are various handles around the button and clicking and dragging one of the handles with alter its size. If you right-click on the button and choose **Format AutoShape** from the context menu, you can scale the button, accurately position it and change the colour.

You don't have to use one of the standard buttons. If you prefer you can make a button from a picture. Go to the **Insert** menu and go down to **Picture**. You may choose a picture from either the built-in clip-art library or a picture of your own.

When you have chosen your picture and located it on the slide, you can then convert it into a button in exactly the same way as you would with one of the standard buttons: by applying an action to it.

5 A new presentation

Action

Right-click on the button and choose **Action Settings...** from the context menu.

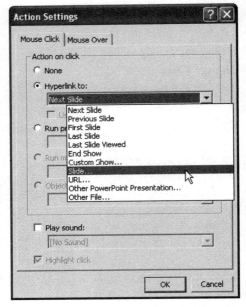

Click the **Hyperlink** radio button and choose the name of the slide you wish to link to from the list of slides, which can include another presentation.

If you choose **Slide...** then a second dialog opens listing all of the slides in the current presentation. The name given to each slide is taken from the title of the slide. If, as is the case here, several slides carry the same title, then refer to the thumbnail on the right of the dialog to locate the slide you wish to link to.

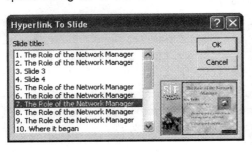

You will observe that there are many actions that a button may perform, including linking to a file from another application.

56

Automatic control

There is a third method of moving between slides and that is automatically. If, for example, you are providing an un-staffed information service that members of the public simply look at, then you can set the presentation to scroll automatically. You need to do two things to get this to work...

- set the time each slide is displayed
- 'tell' the presentation that it is to run automatically

Timing

To set the time, go to the **Slide Show** menu and choose **Slide Transition** to open a dialog.

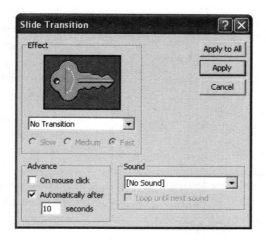

In the area headed **Advance**, tick the box labelled **Automatically after** and enter the number of seconds. The precise duration will clearly depend on how much the viewer has to read. There's only one thing more frustrating than waiting an unnecessarily long period of time for the next slide to appear, and that's finding that the slides change before you get to the bottom which means you've got to wait for the cycle to start again so that you can read all the bottoms of the slides.

5   A new presentation

Having entered the time for each screen to appear, you must 'tell' the presentation that that is how you intend it to be run. Go to the **Slide Show** menu and choose **Set Up Show...** to open a dialog.

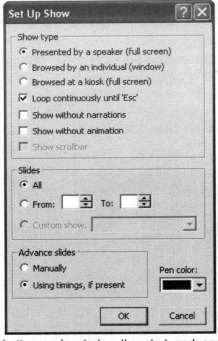

At the bottom is an area headed **Advance slides**. This should be set to **Using timings, if present**.

At the top, under **Show type**, the fourth caption is **Loop continuously until 'Esc'**. This means that when the presentation has got to the end, it will automatically restart and continue to run until the escape key is pressed. Clearly this was specifically included for automatic running.

You will notice that you can automatically show just part of the whole presentation by clicking the **From:** radio button and entering the start and end slide numbers. Alternatively, selecting **Custom show:** with allow you to enter specific slide numbers that will be part of the automatic slide show. For example, 1, 2, 4, 27, 6, 18, etc.

Click the **OK** button to fix the settings.

When the presentation is run, the slides will be automatically displayed in the pre-set order.

Automatic presentation

You may be tempted to incorporate the automatic slide feature into the presentation to accompany your talk. On the face of it, the benefits seem enormous: you can concentrate on what you're saying and leave the computer to run itself.

The reality is that this is a much harder way to give a Presentation as the timing will have to be impeccable. You will have to time what you are going to say down to the second. If you do not follow those timings exactly, the audience will find themselves looking at one slide and hearing you talking about something quite different.

Notes

You can add notes to your presentation slides so that when the presentation is printed, you get pages with the slide at the top and your notes at the bottom.

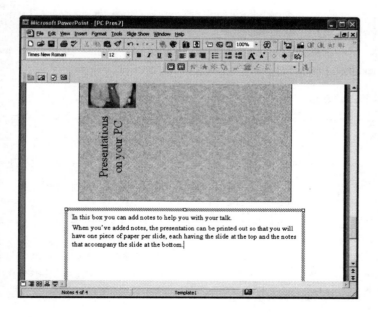

5   A new presentation

A more thorough explanation of this feature is given in Chapter 9 on page 173.

Autorun

Until now, you will have saved your presentation as an editable document which, when first opened will be displayed in a format that can be altered, eg the slide view.

This is not usually the best way to take a presentation to a Presentation. When you are satisfied that everything is exactly how you want it, save it in the usual way, then choose the **Save as...** option from the **File** menu and choose the file type **PowerPoint show**. The new file format will have the icon...

You can keep the same filename, but do not delete the editable file previously saved as alterations will not be able to be made on the 'PowerPoint show' version.

When the presentation is saved in this format, double clicking on the icon will immediately run the presentation as a slideshow.

Alterations

Should you find you need to make any alterations, delete the file with the icon...

... load the file with the icon...

... and make any alterations you need to make. Resave in the usual way and then choose **Save as...** and select the filetype **PowerPoint show** again.

What can be included…

In addition to any buttons (described in the last chapter), a slide can include several elements…

- Text
- Photographs
- Drawings
- Animations
- Video
- Sound
- Charts and Graphs
- Files from other applications

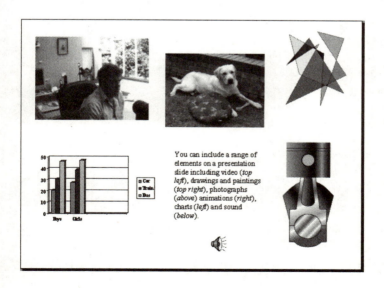

You can include a range of elements on a presentation slide including video (*top left*), drawings and paintings (*top right*), photographs (*above*) animations (*right*), charts (*left*) and sound (*below*).

presentation will determine what elements it

unlikely that many sound files will be included in a
 is designed to accompany a talk or lecture, yet for an
 arning module, files of recorded speech might be an
 rt of the presentation providing verbal instructions without the
te   having to be there in person. It is probably undesirable for a presentation that will be downloaded from the Internet to include many video clips or animations as the resulting file will be too large for most people to download in a sensible time, but these features may be required to demonstrate a point in a presentation to accompany a talk or a learning module.

The next eight chapters (6a to 6h) describe how to apply each of these elements to a slide. It is not envisaged that the reader will plough through each section, just the ones which relate to the elements needed for the presentation currently being worked on.

6a

Text

Words and phrases

All text is entered in a box, (not surprisingly called a text box) which can be positioned anywhere on the slide and even rotated. Most slides give you at least two text boxes: one for the title and one for either a subtitle or body text.

Entering text

Not for nothing does PowerPoint default to 44pt text for the titles and 32pt for the remainder of the text. By comparison, a word processor defaults to 12pt or even 10pt text size for body text. The message is clear: place small quantities of text on each slide and keep the text large so that everyone can see it - even those at the back of the theatre.

If you wish to change text size, first click on the text you wish to change which will highlight the text box with a frame made from hatched lines, and then click  on the actual frame and the hatched lines will change to dots. You can now change the size and style of the text contained in that text box, as well as several other effects.

If you follow these instructions, the change you apply will be applied to all the text in the text box. If you wish to apply a change of size or style to just one word then simply double click on the word to highlight it and then choose the style or effect you want.

6a Text

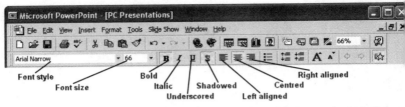

Another way of quickly altering the text size, having selected the appropriate text box, is to click on the large letter **A** on the toolbar to increase the text size by 4 pts or the small **A** to decrease it by 4 pts.

Text style

The actual font style or typeface can have a dramatic effect on the presentation. The default text style is Arial which is a simple design, easily read, but which can look rather formal. Even more formal is Times which, because of its serifs, some people claim is easier to read.

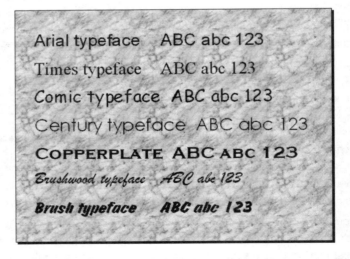

Comic is a popular font which gives the impression of informality although it is easily read. Some fonts are too thin to be used successfully. Century, for example is a clear typeface on paper, but does not always project well.

Text 6a

Capital letters are also thought to be less easily read and so fonts that use all capitals, like Copperplate, are best avoided.

Many fancy script fonts are all but impossible to read. Brushwood is one example although, because of its weight, Brush is better but it should be used sparingly.

Adding a text box

Additional text boxes can be added to a slide by going to the **Insert** menu and choosing **Text box**. The menu will now close and you place the text box by clicking from one corner to the corner diagonally opposite. When you release the mouse button, the text box will be placed and highlighted by a hatched frame with the text cursor positioned inside, on the left. Initially the text box is one line high but as you type it will increase its depth to accommodate more lines of text.

You can move the text box by clicking on a hatched area and dragging it into position. Its size can be adjusted by dragging one of the eight nodes on the edge of the box.

Text box effects

By default, a PowerPoint text box is transparent with no frame. In most cases this is ideal, as it will enable the viewer to see what is under the frame. For example, if you have a light picture or pattern as a background to the slide you will be able to see all of the background except where the actual letters appear.

6a Text

There are occasions, however, when the background is so intense that the letters are actually obscured. This can happen with 'material' backgrounds like marble or stone. For these occasions, add a background colour to the text box to make the text stand out.

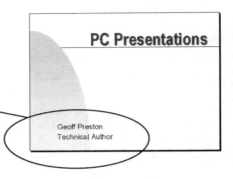

The name and subtitle have been placed in a text box with a transparent background so that the pattern underneath the text can be clearly seen.

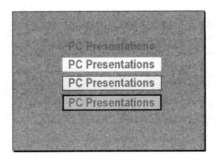

The text at the top is not easy to see against the marbled background. Giving the text box a colour immediately makes it more readable although it does obliterate the background. A frame can improve the text box further. Frames can be applied in a variety of weights including thick and thin lines as shown at the bottom.

Making a text box opaque generally works well if placed over a photograph.

To alter a text box, right click on it to open a context menu and choose **Format AutoShape** to open a dialog.

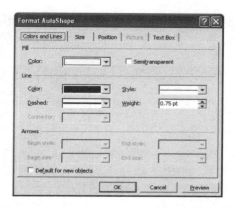

Of the five tabs at the top of the dialog, only four are available (the **Picture** tab being greyed out). Click on the **Colors and Lines** tab to open the dialog where you can change the attributes of the text box. At the top is the **Fill** option, which is initially set to **No fill**. Click the downward facing arrow alongside **Color:** and choose the colour for the text box from the palette. Alongside is a tickbox labelled **Semitransparent**. Ticking this will apply the colour of your choice but will also allow you to see what is under the text box, albeit faded.

In the area headed **Line** you may choose a line colour to surround the text box, which is initially set to **No line**. You may also choose a line style by clicking on the downward facing arrow alongside **Style:** and choosing a style from the list. Similarly the **Weight:** of line may be selected although this must be a multiple of 0.25pt.

On the left is **Dashed:** and this gives a choice of dotted and dashed lines.

To help maintain a degree of consistency, if you think you're likely to add lots of text boxes and you want them to carry the same attributes, tick the **Default for new objects** box.

6a Text

The **Size** tab allows you to set the exact height and width of the text box by entering a number rather that dragging the box and sizing it visually.

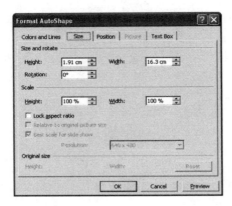

The **Lock aspect ratio** tickbox ensures that the ratio of length to height remains constant regardless of what sizes you enter.

For the majority of users the most important element of this dialog will be the box labelled **Rotation:**. The number of degrees you enter will rotate the text box by that amount in a clockwise direction. Convention has it that text should normally be read from the bottom or from the right, thus enabling people to read the words without twisting their heads to strange angles. To read text from the right, you would have to enter an angle of 270°.

The **Position** tab enables you to accurately position the text box by entering its **Horizontal:** and **Vertical:** position relative to either the **Top Left Corner** or the **Centre** of the box.

Text 6a

The final tab is headed **Text Box** and enables you to determine the position of text within the box. You may declare the distance between the edge of the box and the text on all four sides by entering a value in one of the four boxes labelled **Left:**, **Right:**, **Top:** and **Bottom:**.

You can also determine whether the text is anchored. The default is **Top** which means any space within the text box (i.e. not occupied with text) will be at the bottom of the text box.

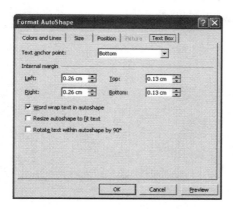

Anchoring the text at the bottom means that text will appear at the bottom and be gradually pushed up as more lines of text are entered.

There is also the option of aligning the text on the left, centre or right.

Underneath are three tick boxes. **Word wrap text in autoshape** means that when you get to the end of a line a new line will be generated automatically. **Resize autoshape to fit text** means that if more text is added, or the size of the text is altered, the size of the text box will be adjusted to suit. An alternative way of rotating the text is to tick the box labelled **Rotate text within autoshape by 90°**. This will rotate the text within the selected text box by 90° (rather than rotating the textbox itself) and may require the text box to be resized. To get the text to be rotated so that it can be read from the right, turn the text box 'inside out'. In other words, drag the bottom edge up past the top edge.

6a Text

Text tips

- Much of the text placed on a slide will be bulleted points, and some of the slide layouts are set up to provide such a list.
- Do not put lots of text (i.e. paragraph after paragraph) onto a slide.
- Keep to large sizes to ensure text can be read easily.
- Avoid ornate fonts.

6b
Photographs

A picture, it is said, is worth a thousand words. Including a picture in a presentation can not only add to the information on a slide, but can also make the overall appearance of a slide less intimidating.

But before you can include a picture, you need to capture it. The main methods are...

- Digital camera
- Scanning a photograph
- Capturing from the web

Having captured a picture you may need to do some work on it before it can be included in your presentation.

Digital camera

The cost of digital cameras has fallen very significantly although they are still more expensive than traditional film cameras. But you don't have to spend a fortune - you can get some very acceptable pictures with one of the new generation of miniature digital cameras like this Blink which is about 2 inches square. They offer

several benefits over film cameras, including almost zero running costs as there is no film and no developing.

Most digital cameras output pictures as JPEGs (Joint Photographic Experts Group) which is the format used by most presentation creation applications.

6b Photographs

Scanning a photograph

Pictures previously taken with a film camera can be used in a presentation providing you have a scanner to create a digital image from the picture. Colour scanners are remarkably cheap and easy to use, whilst giving excellent results - certainly as good as the pictures taken with a cheap digital camera.

Unless you intend scanning a picture you have personally shot, then you should be aware that there may be a copyright issue. This is particularly true of pictures scanned from books, magazines and newspapers.

Capturing from the web

Again, beware of copyright rules which may apply to some pictures on the Internet. Downloading a picture couldn't be simpler. Once you've found the picture you want, right-click on it to open a context menu. Choose **Save Picture as...** and save the picture in the location you want and with the filename of your choice.

If the picture is in JPEG format, it's ready to use as it is. If it's in another format you may need to convert it before you can place in into your presentation. Paint, which is supplied with Microsoft Windows, can handle several formats. Right-click on the file and choose **Open with...** from the context menu. When you've got the file into Paint, choose **Save as...** from the **File** menu and save it as a JPEG by choosing the correct option from the list of possible file types.

Preparing pictures

Although it's possible to include a picture 'as is', it's likely you will want to make some alterations to it first. Welcome to the world of digital image editing. Like so many aspects of creating a presentation, this is a subject of its own and so only a small part of it can be included.

Some of this work can be done with MS Paint which is supplied with Windows. However, if you intend doing a lot of this type of work then it will be worth getting an application intended for digital picture imaging. Scanners and cameras are frequently supplied with free software to enable you to do this type of work and although free, these are usually very capable applications which will enable you to do basic editing as well as a variety of special effects.

Of all the picture editing exercises you could do for a presentation, the three most common are...

- Cropping a picture
- Improving the photograph
- Adding a border

Cropping a picture

It's unlikely that you would want to use a picture exactly how it came out of the camera or scanner. In most cases the picture would need to be trimmed or cropped. Apart from reducing its physical size, cropping removes some of the actual picture (just as trimming a printed photograph would remove some of the picture) and it will also reduce the amount of memory it occupies. The latter may be an issue if you want to transport your presentation from one computer to another.

Most photo editing or retouching programs require you to choose the selection tool, drag a rectangle over the area you wish to keep and choose **Crop** which can often be found in the **Edit** menu.

6b   Photographs

Every photo editing program I've ever seen includes the facility to crop pictures, but if you haven't got such a program, you can use Paint although it's a little more involved.

On the right is not the best photograph in the world, but I'm not the best photographer in the world. There is no reason why the subject should be in the centre, but to save space on the presentation slide, the section on the left is to be removed. Once the photograph has been opened in Paint, choose the rectangle selection tool which is at the top right of the toolbox.

Select the area of the picture you wish to keep by dragging a rectangle over the picture. It's usually best to begin at the top left and drag down to the bottom right.

Next, move the mouse pointer into the middle of the selected area and drag it to the top left. Get the picture as tight into the corner as possible so as not to leave any of the unwanted picture showing above or to the left.

74

Photographs 6b

Finally, move the mouse pointer to the node at the bottom right of the picture and drag it up and to the left to reduce the physical size of the picture, thus removing all the picture except for the area which was originally selected.

The picture can now be resaved and will be ready to include in your presentation slide. Note that Paint will save the file in the same format as it was in when opened (e.g. BMP, JPG, etc.)

Paint can handle many photo formats, although most will have to be opened by right-clicking on the photo file icon and choosing **Open with...** from the context menu. From there you should be able to choose Paint.

Improving the photograph

If your photo skills are as good as mine, then you'll frequently find that you will need to adjust the colour, contrast, brightness or tone of a picture. Again, a small amount of adjustment is possible in Paint, but this task really does need a good photo editing program.

Many scanners and digital cameras are supplied with photo editing software but if you don't have one there are several good but relatively cheap examples on the market such as *Photo Explosion* by Nova and *PhotoPlus* by Serif, both of which are available from high-street computer stores.

Without doubt, it is better to have a photograph that doesn't require any adjustment, but it is surprising what some of this software can do to make a bad photo look better.

6b Photographs

Adding a border

A border or frame on a picture can make it stand out, especially if you are using a pattern effect as the background to a slide.

Many programs offer a huge range of frames, but adding a simple border is well within the capabilities of Paint.

With the picture opened in Paint, choose the **Magnifier** tool and enlarge the picture.

Select the **Straight line** tool and draw a line around the edge of the picture. If the edge of the picture is quite dark and it's going to be displayed on a dark background, choose a light colour for the border. If you have a large picture which will be scaled down when displayed on the slide, you may need to draw two lines side by side, or even three or four.

Although this may seem a slightly tedious exercise, it really is worth doing as is will dramatically improve the appearance of photographs.

Of course, you don't have to stick to a single line. You could, for example, add two thick black lines, a white line and then another black line.

Inserting pictures

To insert a photograph into a slide, go to the **Insert** menu, go down to **Picture** and choose **From File...** to open an explorer dialog.

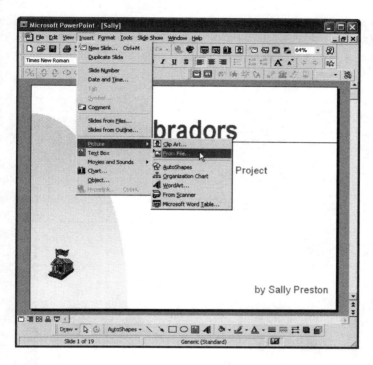

Locate the file you wish to use and click the **Insert** button on the right of the dialog. This will place the picture on the slide.

To change the size of the picture you may either drag one of the nodes at the corners or the centre of the edges, or right click on the picture to open a context menu from where you choose **Format picture...** . In the **Format Picture** dialog, select the **Size** tab and set the picture size by typing in a percentage of the full size picture. For example, 50% will display the picture half size, although it will still use the same amount of memory. This does not reduce the size of the picture, only the size at which it is displayed.

6b Photographs

If the picture size is adjusted from the **Format Picture** dialog, ensure the **Lock aspect ratio** button is ticked if you want to keep the height to width proportions constant.

Click once on the picture and the resizing nodes will be displayed. Dragging the nodes on the edge of the picture with re-scale the picture, but note that the nodes on the edges will not maintain the picture's aspect ratio. If you want to preserve the aspect ratio, use the nodes on the corners.

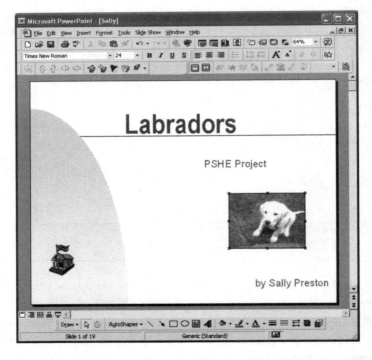

Do not attempt to enlarge a small picture as this will lead to an effect known as pixelation. In simple terms, the tiny dots that make up the picture become enlarged and the picture takes on a chunky appearance.

Photographs 6b

To position the picture, move the mouse pointer into the centre and drag it into the required position.

Backgrounds

A trick that is frequently used in presentations is to use a picture in the background that has been faded so that you can still recognise what it is, but it doesn't detract from the text placed on top of it.

The way to achieve this in PowerPoint is to use a feature called **Watermark**.

Open the Master Slide by going to the **View** menu, moving down to **Master** and choosing **Slide Master** from the sub menu. Insert the picture you want for your background as previously described.

You now have three things to do. First is to scale it so that it fits the area you want it to cover. This may be the whole slide or just part of it.

Next, click the right button over the picture to open a context menu from where you choose **Format Picture...** to open a dialog.

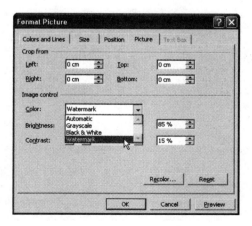

Choose **Watermark** from the **Picture** tab and click the **OK** button the make the picture appear faded.

6b Photographs

Finally, right-click on the picture and choose **Order** and then **Send to Back** to place the picture behind all of the other objects such as text boxes and other pictures.

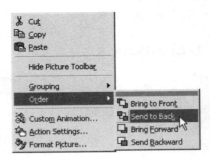

All slides that are added to the presentation will now have the watermark at the back.

If you want a picture that fills the whole slide, and you don't want to stretch it either horizontally or vertically, then you'll need a picture which has the same aspect ratio as the slide. Normally this will be 4:3.

6c
Drawings

Most presentation applications allow you to import drawings (this is described in Chapter 6h on page 137), but before attempting to do that, find out what drawing facilities your presentation application has available. It is unlikely that any on-board drawing facilities will be as extensive as those found in a professional drawing application, but there might be enough to enable you to do what you want.

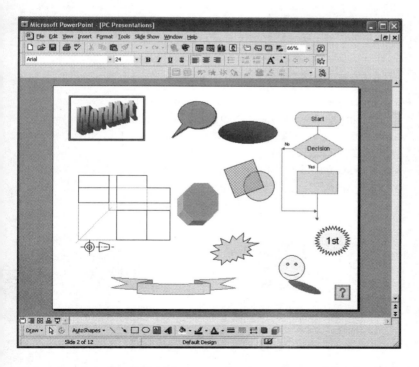

As you can see, PowerPoint has an extensive armoury of drawing tools that can be used to create all manner of diagrams and charts.

6c Drawings

Before attempting to begin any type of drawing in PowerPoint you must first make the appropriate toolbar visible. If the drawing toolbar is not visible, go to the **View** menu, go down to **Toolbars** and click **Drawing**. This will place a tick by the menu entry and place the toolbar somewhere in the PowerPoint window. As with other toolbars, the Drawing toolbar may be added to the top, bottom, left or right of the window, or left as a floating object as shown here.

(To move the toolbar to a different location, position the mouse pointer on the blue header of the floating toolbar, or the double lines on a fixed toolbar, and simply drag it to a new position.)

Drawing control

The graphics used in PowerPoint are known as object-oriented graphics which simply means that a drawing is made up from individual components called objects. Each object can be moved around independently by dragging them into position. They can also be moved forward and back so that one object can be placed in front of or behind another object.

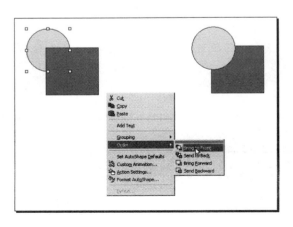

Drawings   6c

On the left of the picture opposite, the light circle is clearly behind the dark square. Right-clicking on the circle will select it and open a context menu. Go down to **Order** and choose **Bring to Front**. The result is shown on the right where the circle is now in front of the square. Objects can be moved either to the front or back, or re-ordered using the **Bring Forward** and **Send Backward** options. This is the equivalent of moving the position of one card in a pack of cards.

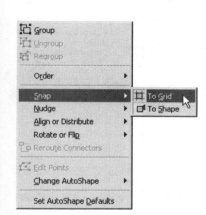

Grid

To enable objects to be located more accurately, you should enable the snap to grid feature. Click the **Draw** button on the Drawing toolbar, go to **Snap** and choose **To Grid.** This will ensure that when you draw two objects that should touch, they will touch exactly. For example, two lines that are supposed to meet to form an angle will actually form the angle rather than crossing over each other, or missing each other altogether.

Group

Several objects may be grouped together so that they behave as one. Select the objects you wish to group by clicking on the first one and then Shift-clicking subsequent objects (i.e. holding down the Shift key whilst clicking). When you have selected all the objects you wish to group, right-click on one of them to open a context menu. Go down to

Grouping and choose **Group** from the sub menu. When selecting small or thin shapes such as lines, ensure that the mouse pointer is exactly

6c Drawings

over the shape. When you are in position, the mouse point should change to a cross.

Align and Distribute

Regardless of any grid setting you may have, objects can be aligned so that they are, for example, centred or distributed so that there is an even space between them.

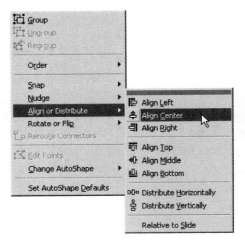

To align objects you must normally select at least two and then click the **Draw** button on the Drawing toolbar, go to **Align or Distribute** and choose one of the six alignment options, which includes a thumbnail to show you precisely what you can expect from each option.

To distribute you normally have to select at least three objects. The outer two (i.e. the one at the very top and very bottom, or those on the extreme left or right) will remain in the same place whilst those in between will be moved so that there is an equal space between them.

If you select the bottom menu option, **Relative to Slide**, then only one object need be selected and any subsequent alignment or distribution will be relative to the slide thus enabling objects to be centred not only relative to each other, but centred on the slide too. This will almost always mean that all selected objects will move to some extent.

If using either of these features it is important not to attempt to move them after. If you do, the only way you'll get them back into exactly the same position is to re-align or re-distribute them because once they have been moved they will lock back onto the grid which may not be aligned in the same way.

Drawings 6c

Objects

Every component of a drawing is referred to as an object, (or in PowerPoint parlance, an AutoShape) and can be controlled in the same way. There are basically two types of object...

- Lines
- Shapes

Lines

A line may be drawn anywhere on a slide and be given one or more of the following properties...

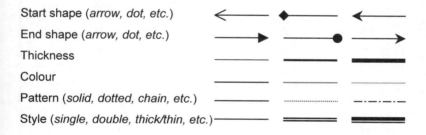

Start shape (*arrow, dot, etc.*)
End shape (*arrow, dot, etc.*)
Thickness
Colour
Pattern (*solid, dotted, chain, etc.*)
Style (*single, double, thick/thin, etc.*)

These attributes may be applied before the line is drawn, but it is usually much easier to apply them after. You may draw and then select several lines if you wish to apply the same attributes to all of them.

Having selected the line or lines, some of the attributes may be selected from the **Drawing** toolbar.

For a more comprehensive selection of attributes, move the mouse pointer onto one of them and right-click to open a context menu. From the context menu choose **Format AutoShape...** to open a dialog.

6c Drawings

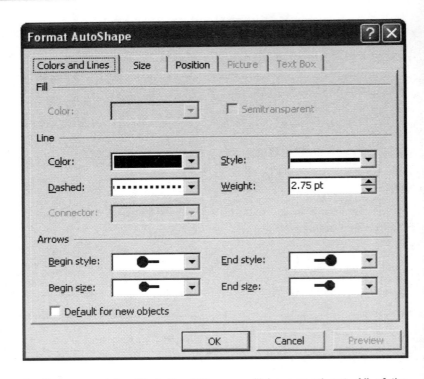

As lines cannot be filled, the **Fill** area will be greyed out. All of the options are chosen by clicking the downward facing arrow alongside each of the options and selecting the attribute you want applied to the selected line or lines. Clicking **OK** will apply the selected attributes and close the dialog.

If you wish, you may tick the **Default for new objects** box in which case all new objects (lines and shapes) will inherit the selected attributes.

The **Size** tab allows you to adjust sizes by giving them a numeric dimension. Similarly clicking the **Position** tab will enable you to accurately position lines by entering a distance from either the top left corner or the centre of the slide.

Note that some of these options will not be available if more than one object has been selected.

Drawings 6c

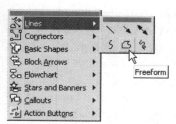

Apart from straight lines, you may also draw freehand lines and connected lines. Click the **AutoShape** button on the **Drawing** toolbar and go to **Lines** to open a sub menu with six options.

The meaning of the top three is self-evident: the bottom three may require some explanation.

The squiggly line on the bottom left works in the same way as a straight line except that you may draw several connected lines and each will be curved so that you get a smooth transition between the lines. If you finish drawing in the same place you started the shape will be closed and could then be given a fill colour.

The button at the bottom centre allows you to draw straight connected lines. Again, if you finish in the same place as you started, the shape will be closed and could then be filled. To draw a shape, click the mouse button where you want a corner to be placed. If you hold the left mouse button you will draw a freehand curve.

The bottom right option will enable you to draw a completely freehand line which will form a closed shape if you finish drawing in the same place as you began. To draw using this tool, hold the mouse button down to draw, and release it to stop drawing.

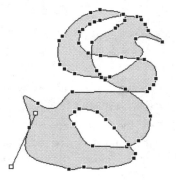

When a shape has been completed you may edit it by right-clicking on it and choosing **Edit Points** from the context menu. This will place a series of points around the shape which can be dragged into a new position. If the point is on a curve, two additional points will appear which can be dragged to adjust the curve.

87

6c Drawings

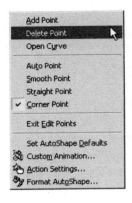

Further adjustment and editing may be carried out by right-clicking on one of the points to open a context menu. You can change the type of point to a corner or a curve and smooth the point so that you get a smooth transition between the two lines. Additional points can be added and those that exist can be deleted.

The third option from the top allows you to open a closed shape so that it becomes a line, or if the shape is already open, it can be closed.

Shapes

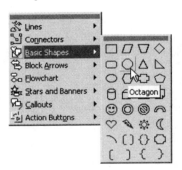

The way shapes are positioned is much the same as for lines, except that you draw a shape by plotting diagonally opposite corners. Select the shape you want to draw from the **Drawing** toolbar, click roughly where you want one corner to be and, whilst holding the left mouse button, drag to the diagonally opposite corner. If you want to draw a perfect square (as opposed to a rectangle) or a perfect circle (as opposed to an ellipse), hold the Shift key whilst dragging. Once the object has been drawn, it can be dragged into position.

The two shapes provided on the toolbar are the most common and widely used shapes, but there are others - over 150 others.

Click the **AutoShape** button on the **Drawing** toolbar and a menu with eight options is opened. Each leads to a sub menu with up to 32 shapes. Choose the one you want and draw it in the way previously described.

Drawings 6c

Apart from changing the attributes of the lines, you can select the fill colour from the **Format AutoShape** dialog. You can also set the line colour and fill colour from the buttons on the **Drawing** toolbar.

The downward facing arrow alongside each of the tools leads to a menu from where you may select the colour or style. Clicking the actual tool sets that attribute to the selected object.

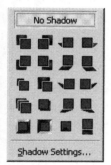

Two further effects may be applied to a shape. On the right of the **Drawing** toolbar are two buttons for **Shadow** and **3D effect**.

Each of these leads to a menu from where you can choose the effect you want from a range of pre-set shadows or 3D effects. To use one of these effects, select the shape by clicking on it once, and then selecting the effect from the appropriate menu. If the effects provided on either of the menus is not to your exact requirements, click on the button at the bottom (labelled **Shadow Settings...** or **3-D Settings...**) to open a toolbar from which you may select from a range of options to create the exact effect required. In the case of **3D Settings...** you can rotate the object about a vertical and horizontal axis to get the proportions correct. You can choose the direction of a light source, which will put different faces into light and shadow, and you can choose the material from which the object is made.

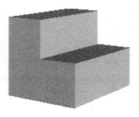

89

6c Drawings

Examples

The examples shown on page 81 were all created using PowerPoint's on-board drawing features.

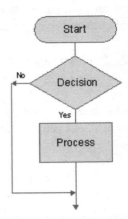

The flowchart on the right is created with shape objects from the **Flowchart AutoShapes** menu, straight lines (with and without arrowheads) and text boxes. Draw a shape, insert a text box, add the text label, align them and group them. Do this with all of the boxes required for your flowchart. (To ensure boxes of a similar type are exactly the same size, draw one then copy (CTRL+C) and Paste (CTRL+V).) Select all boxes which are intended to be underneath each other, centre align them and then distribute so they are equally spaced. Draw lines between them and put them to the back so that if they should be slightly too long, they won't intrude into the boxes. Finally, align the lines so they are central to the boxes.

The orthographic drawing is made up mainly from shapes, lines and closed lines. The advantage of using closed shapes is that they can be coloured.

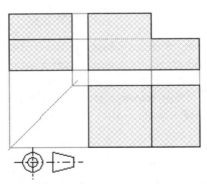

The simple orthographic drawing on the left is basically four boxes (two for the plan on the bottom right and two for the elevation on the left). The front elevation is a closed line drawing. The projection lines are really superfluous as the locked grid ensures objects will line up perfectly but have been drawn and placed behind to show how projection works. In order to see the projection lines in the front elevation, the fill colours have been made semi-transparent.

6d
Animations

In addition to the animated effects available in most presentation applications, it is also usually possible to include animated pictures on the presentation slides.

There are two reasons why you might want to include animations in a presentation...

- To draw attention to a particular point.
- To explain how a process works.

The principle behind creating a computer-generated animation is exactly the same as for hand-drawn animations: produce a number of pictures and display them in quick succession to give the illusion of movement.

File types

Different presentation applications use different combinations of animation file types and it may be that the animation file type you want to use cannot be imported into your presentation. Before embarking on some fairly time-consuming work, first check what animation files your presentation application supports. If the presentation application you are using does not support the animation file type you want to use, check if there is a plug-in or software add-on which will enable your presentation application to read additional file types.

The two main animation file types, which can be displayed by most presentation applications, are AVI and animated GIF. Some software like Serif *PhotoPlus* can import in one format and export in another effectively converting the file format.

6d Animations

Creating animations

Animations can be created with a variety of drawing and painting programs. Which one you use will probably depend on exactly what you're trying to achieve. For most purposes, Serif's *DrawPlus* will be perfectly adequate. *DrawPlus* is a drawing program that has the option of creating animations. Although the explanation given here is for *DrawPlus*, the principle is much the same for most programs.

The smallest number of frames that can be used to create an animation is two, although in reality you usually need a few more to get a smooth animation. As it is not possible to show animations in a book, the examples shown here can be found on my website at www.word4word.uk.com/.

Highlights

It's easy to create little cartoons that can be positioned to draw the viewer's attention to a point. To demonstrate this, we are going to create a moving arrow that will shift from side to side and will be placed alongside a piece of text instead of a bullet.

Open *DrawPlus* and choose **Create an Animation** from the wizard.

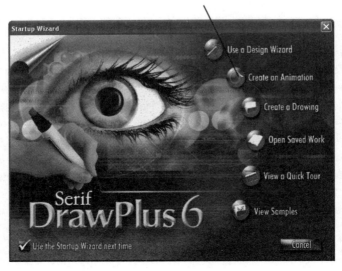

Animations 6d

This will open a dialog giving you the opportunity to choose the size for your animation. Choose **Add Page Size...** and create a new page size of 100 pixels square. Then click the **Finish** button.

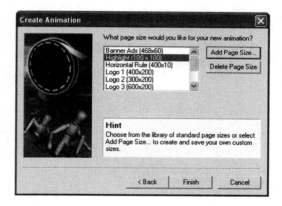

This will open a drawing which, although it may appear to be rather large, will have been scaled up.

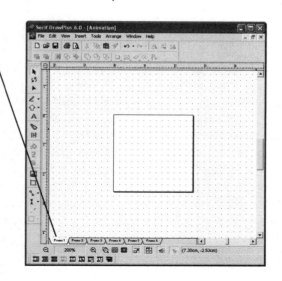

6d   Animations

Initially the animation will have just 1 frame, but right-clicking on the frame number at the bottom left of the window will open a context menu from which you can add additional frames. After adding 5 frames, click on the **Frame 1** tab and draw the picture for your first frame. Do not fill the frame with the picture: you must leave some room to allow it to move by drawing as far to the left as possible.

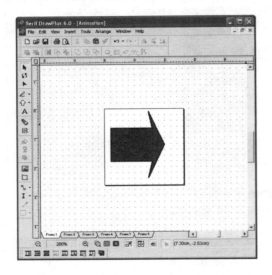

Having drawn the first frame, select it by clicking on it and then press CTRL+C to copy it into a special area of memory called the clipboard. Click on the **Frame 2** tab and paste the picture into the second frame by pressing CTRL+V. There are two reasons for doing it this way. First, having drawn the first frame, copying and pasting saves you the trouble of having to re-draw it. Secondly, using copy and paste ensures that the image you have in frame 1 will be the same as in frame 2. When the picture is pasted into the second frame it will be in exactly the same position as it is in the first frame. Move the image slightly to the right, then copy and paste it into the third frame.

Animations 6d

Some animation programs (DrawPlus included) has the option to clone a frame, which basically duplicates the frame, and its contents in one go.

Do the same with frame three: copy and paste it into the fourth frame and then move it slightly to the right.

When you get to the fifth frame, drag the picture to the left instead of the right. Similarly the sixth frame, drag it to the left. In fact, the fifth frame will be exactly the same as the third frame and the sixth frame will be the same as the second.

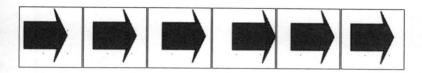

When the animation is run as an endless loop, the frame order will be 1, 2, 3, 4, 5, 6, 1, 2, etc. As you can see, the arrow will start at the left, move to the right and then come back again.

Rotation

The minimum number of frames required to show rotation is three. Two frames will make the movement appear to oscillate.

The way to achieve this is to divide the angle between two adjacent objects by 3.

The picture shows a frame containing a single image of eight dots. The angle between the dots is 45°. (360° divided by 8.) Divide 45° by 3 and you get 15°. The second frame should then be rotated by 15° and the third frame by a further 15°. For a small animation (e.g. 100 pixels square) this is acceptable. For anything larger you would need to

6d Animations

reduce the distance between the elements. (In this case that would mean either beginning with more dots or using more frames to get a smooth and convincing movement.)

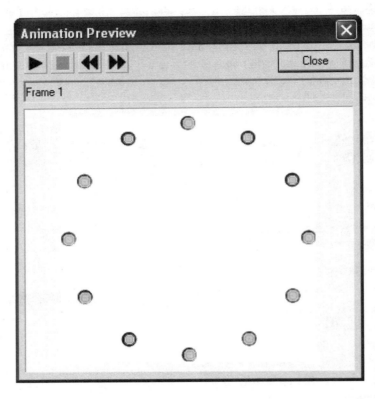

Twelve dots and a rotational distance of 5° gives 6 frames and makes for a much more convincing animation.

Saving

Most animation programs can save files in either native format (i.e. the format peculiar to that program) or other general formats like AVI and GIF. Regardless of what format you need for your presentation, always save it in native format so that you can edit it later.

Animations 6d

Placing the animation

When you have saved your animation in a format that can be used by your presentation application you are ready to insert it onto a slide.

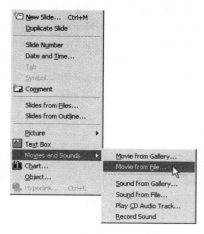

Display the slide on which you want to place your animation, go to the **Insert** menu, move down to **Movies and Sounds** and choose **Movies from file...** to open the standard file dialog.

Choose the animation file you wish to place and click **OK** to insert it.

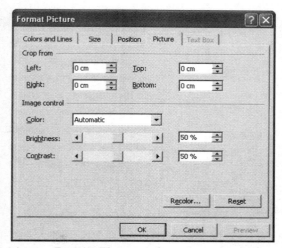

When the animation is on the slide, you will only see the first frame. To see it play, double-click on it.

The size and position can then be adjusted in exactly the same way as for a still picture or photograph - right click on the animation and choose **Format Picture...** from the context menu. You can also adjust the size by dragging the handles on the edges of the animation frame or move it around on the slide by dragging.

6d Animations

Controlling the animation

Depending on the type of presentation and/or how you intend giving the presentation will determine how the animation or animations will run. The options are...

- Run when the mouse is clicked over it.
- Run when the mouse is moved over it.
- Automatically run when the slide is opened (or after a pre-determined interval).

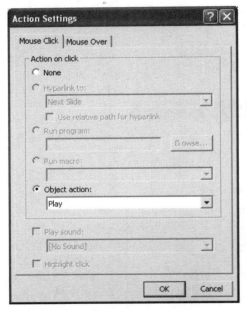

Right-click on the animation and choose **Action settings** from the context menu to open a dialog. The two tabs provide you with control for **Mouse Click** and **Mouse Over**. In most cases you would want to choose one or the other, and in the appropriate dialog, check the **Object action:** button and choose **Play** from the drop-down menu.

Click **OK** to set the action and close the dialog.

To set the animation to begin automatically when the slide is open, right-click over the animation and choose **Custom Animation...** from the context menu to open a dialog.

Animations 6d

In the **Timing** tab, click on the **Animate** radio button and then the button labelled **Automatically**.

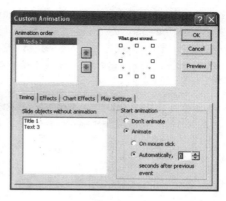

You may then enter a number of seconds after the previous animation event to begin this animation. If zero is entered, the animation will begin immediately the slide is displayed.

By clicking the **Play Settings** tab you may choose to pause all other events whilst the animation is playing, or continue with other events (e.g. other animations, sound files, etc.) whilst it is playing.

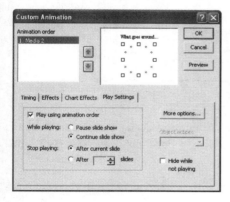

Be aware that too many animations running at the same time may cause all of them to slow down, or even stop. Exactly how many animations can be run simultaneously will depend on the size of each animation (i.e. both the frame size and the number of frames in the animation) and the power or speed of the computer being used to run the presentation.

The entry at the bottom left is labelled **Stop playing:** and provides you with the opportunity to stop the animation after the current slide has been replaced or later. The purpose of this is to stop sound files or animations which contain sounds from playing for too long.

6d Animations

On the right is a button labelled **More options...** and clicking this opens a dialog offering you the choice of looping the animation and/or rewinding it so that if it is played again, it will begin at the beginning rather than continuing from where it was stopped.

Click **OK** to close the **Play Options** dialog.

When you return to the **Custom Animation** dialog, there is the option to preview your work, but this generally does not work well with small animations.

Click **OK** to close the dialog to fix the settings.

Creating large animations

Using exactly the same technique as previously outlined, it is possible to create a large animation to explain a particular effect or process. Teachers will find this facility particularly useful for class presentations.

Before embarking on what could be a large amount of work, check first that the computer you are going to use is capable of running the large scale (potentially full-screen) animations at a sensible speed. You will need a fast processor and plenty of memory to get it to run smoothly. If the computer has to work near to its maximum processing ability, you

Animations 6d

could end up with a series of still pictures rather than a smooth and convincing animation.

The first frame

You will need to begin by creating a blank frame. The actual size is not important although it should be no larger than full screen size. If you are going to fill the screen, remember the aspect ratio (the ratio of height to width) should be 4:3 which is the same aspect ratio as a computer monitor. If you choose a frame size which is very much smaller than the screen size you may have to scale it up to fit onto the slide which could degrade the quality of the drawings. A frame size which is too large is pointless because it will require more processing power to run, even though you'll have to scale it down to fit on the slide.

Having established the size of the frame, begin drawing the first picture. Each part of an animation frame is a separate object that can be moved independently of all others.

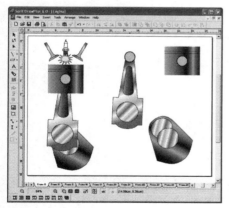

The animation showing how a 4-stroke internal combustion engine works, basically has three main components: the piston (which moves up and down), the crankshaft (which rotates) and the connecting rod (which connects the piston to the crankshaft).

In each new frame, the crankshaft is rotated 15°, the connecting rod rotated and re-positioned so that the big end connects to the crankshaft and the small end remains in the centre. The piston is then placed in the correct position on the connecting rod.

Because the crankshaft is rotated by 15° for each frame, 24 frames are required. However, the full four-stroke cycle requires two revolutions of the crankshaft, making 48 frames for the animation.

6d Animations

As with the small animations that are used for highlights (described at the beginning of this chapter), draw a complete frame (below left) and either copy and paste your drawing into a new frame (below right) or create a clone of the frame. Either way, all the components of the frame will be present and in the same position as the previous frame. You can then make small alterations to the position of the drawn components of the frame.

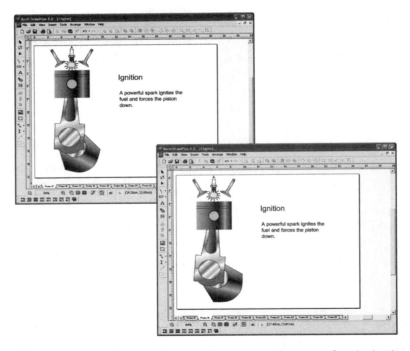

When creating a large-scale animation, you must remember to try to make only small adjustments to the items on the page. Large adjustments will make the animation very jerky. Also, if you want the animation to maintain a constant speed, you must carefully work out how much movement there should be between frames. Large movements will make the movement seem faster (although too fast and it will become jerky) whilst smaller movements will slow down the action.

Animations   6d

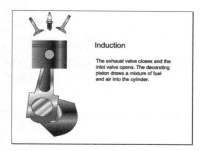
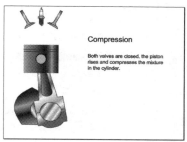

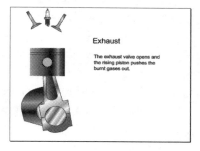

Four of the 48 frames which make up the animation which demonstrates the workings of the 4 stroke internal combustion engine. This animation took about two hours to put together from beginning to end. Drawing programs, like Serif's *DrawPlus* are very easy to use. It even includes a range of fill options which can make steel look like steel and give cylinders a distinctly rounded appearance.

The captions which appear on the right are part of the animation frames but you should only consider doing something like this if your computer is powerful enough to cope with the extra processing it requires. This additional feature more than doubles the file size, because the physical area the animation now occupies is doubled. Without the captions, the frame size of the finished animation would be roughly $^1/_3$ of the area of the screen.

6d Animations

Points to consider

- Even if you are using large-scale animations, keep the size to a minimum to help keep the animation as smooth as possible.
- Small movements between frames slows down the action and can create very large files which older computers may have difficulty handling.
- Large movements between frames will speed up the action but can lead to jerky movements.
- If the reason for the animation is to emphasise a point, then it follows that you should not have many of them on a slide.
- If the purpose of the animation is to explain a process, then do not detract from it by including other animations on the same page.
- As with all clever effects, you need to use animations with care. Do not use lots of moving images on the same slide and resist the temptation to add lots of effects with your animation.

6e
Video

For sheer memory consumption, there's not much to beat a video clip. A 5 second video, captured at 15 frames per second with accompanying sound, will create a file well of over 2 megabytes if recorded in 16-bit colour. (A standard floppy disc is 1.6Mbytes - so the resulting file would be too large to fit on that.) The frame would be roughly $1/9$ the size of the screen. Whilst the quality of the actual picture would be acceptable, it could be a little jumpy if the computer is old and has a slow processor and not much memory. If you want to increase the number of frames to a more acceptable 25 frames per second to get smoother action, increase the size of the frame or improve the colour to 24-bit, then the file size soars and you'll need a fairly powerful computer to run it.

But in spite of those drawbacks, video can be used to great effect in presentations.

How to capture

There are basically three ways to capture video, and each requires additional hardware to be connected to the computer being used to create the presentation, although not to the computer being used to give the presentation. The three methods are...

- from a video camera
- from a live television broadcast
- from a video cassette recorder.

Video camera

Without doubt, the easiest and cheapest way to capture video is with a WebCam, some of which are now incredibly cheap.

6e Video

Most modern WebCams connect to the computer through the Universal Serial Bus (USB). If you're using this connection, it's better to connect

the WebCam directly to the computer and not via a USB hub (a device designed to increase the number of USB ports on a computer). In addition to the camera you'll also need a microphone connected to your computer's sound card if you want to record sound as well as pictures.

Logitech's *Eyeball* WebCam is typical. It is supplied with its own stand but also has a standard camera screw on the bottom so it can be fitted on to a camera tripod. The only adjustment on the camera is the focusing ring around the lens.

Video 6e

The software provides several settings. Having set the image size at the top right of the window, (shown opposite as 320x240) and the number of colours (centre right) clicking the **Record Movie** button will begin recording both sound and video. Clicking the same button again will stop the recording and the file will be saved to a pre-determined location.

Although the quality is good, it will not be as good as video recorded from a camcorder which will feature better focusing, zoom and a variety of aperture settings. Both digital and analogue camcorders can be used to capture video images for inclusion in a presentation, provided you can find a way of connecting the device to the computer.

There are several video capture devices available which enable you to connect your camcorder to your computer and enable you to download the video images stored on the camera's tape and convert it into a file format that can be controlled by your computer.

6e Video

Digital video cameras are easier because the video recorded by the camera is already in the correct format (or at least a computer-readable format) so it only needs to be downloaded from the camera to the computer. To transfer digital video images you are likely to need a Firewire card conforming to IEEE-1394/DV.

Television

There are several television adapters available that can be either fitted into your computer or supplied as an external unit which is connected to the computer via one of the ports provided at the back.

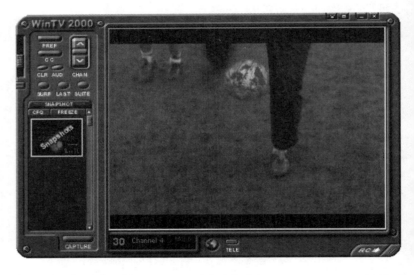

The idea is to enable you to watch television on your computer but software like that supplied with some WebCams enables you to capture the television sound and picture and save it as a file which can be displayed in your presentation.

NB If you intend capturing television pictures be aware that they are subject to copyright.

Video cassette recorder

An interesting spin-off is that most TV adapters are fitted with a selection of ports that enable you to connect a camcorder and download video recordings. You can also connect a VCR (video cassette recorder) and thus capture video clips from pre-recorded video tapes. Once again, be aware of copyright laws.

Placing a video clip

When you have got your video clip saved onto your computer it will usually appear as an AVI file which can be played in any application which supports that format, including most presentation creation tools.

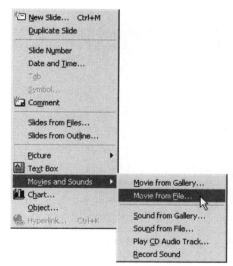

With the slide on which you want to place the video clip, go to the **Insert** menu, go down to **Movies and Sounds** and choose **Movie from file...** to open an explorer dialog.

Navigate through the selection the suitable files, click on the one you want and then click the **OK** button to place the file, which will be displayed with its first frame. You may move the picture into any position on the slide and change its size by dragging one of the nodes on the corners and sides of the picture. If you do attempt to change the size,

6e Video

only do so to make it smaller. If you drag the nodes outwards to increase the picture size you will find the quality could be compromised.

Controlling the video clip

Depending on the type of presentation and/or how you intend giving the presentation will determine how the video or videos will run. The options are...

- Run when the mouse is clicked over it.
- Run when the mouse is moved over it.
- Automatically run when the slide is opened (or after a pre-determined interval).

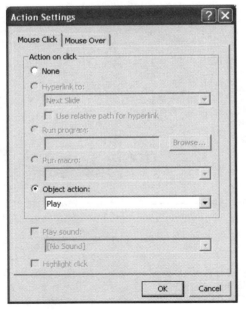

Right-click on the video clip and choose **Action settings** from the context menu to open a dialog. The two tabs provide you with control for **Mouse Click** and **Mouse Over**. In most cases you would want to choose one or the other, and in the appropriate dialog, check the **Object action:** button and choose **Play** from the drop-down menu.

Click **OK** to set the action and close the dialog.

Video 6e

To set the video clip to begin automatically when the slide is open, right-click over the video clip and choose **Custom Animation...** from the context menu to open a dialog.

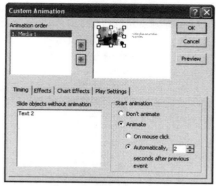

You may then enter a number of seconds after the previous animation event to begin this animation. If zero is entered, the animation will begin immediately the slide is displayed.

By clicking the **Play Settings** tab you may choose to pause all other events whilst the video clip is playing, or continue with other events (e.g. other video clips, sound files, etc.) whilst it is playing.

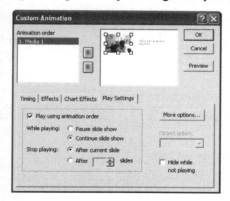

Be aware that too many videos running at the same time may cause all of them to slow down, or even stop. Exactly how many video clips can be run simultaneously will depend on the size of each video file (i.e. both the frame size and the duration of the video file) and the power or speed of the computer being used to run the presentation.

The entry at the bottom left is labelled **Stop playing:** and provides you with the opportunity to stop the video after the current slide has been replaced, or later. The purpose of this is to stop sound files or video clips which contain sound from playing for too long.

6e Video

On the right of the dialog is a button labelled **More options...** and clicking this opens a dialog offering you the choice of looping the video and/or rewinding it so that if it is played again, it will begin at the beginning rather than continuing from where it was stopped.

Click **OK** to close the **Play Options** dialog.

When you return to the **Custom Animation** dialog, there is the option to preview your work.

Click **OK** to close the dialog to fix the settings.

Special effects

As with all animations, if you are using them, use special effects with care or the viewer will be bombarded with action. One effect that works particularly well with video clips is the camera effect which opens the video rather like the shutter of a camera after which is can be made to play automatically.

Sound

This section will probably not be of great interest to those who are preparing a presentation to accompany a live talk or lecture. It is conceivable that recorded sounds may be used in such a presentation but it is more likely that sounds will be used with free-standing presentations and learning modules.

There are four ways of incorporating sound into a presentation...

- as a sound effect used to accompany an action (this is fully described in the section on Special effects on page 150)
- as a pre-recorded file (with or without video)
- input directly into the presentation application
- as an accompanying track from a Music CD.

Pre-recorded sound file

To insert a pre-recorded sound file, go to the **Insert** menu, go down to **Movies and Sounds** and choose **Sound from File...** to open a dialog from which you may search and then select the appropriate sound file.

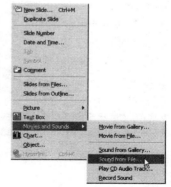

Once it has been placed, a speaker icon will be displayed on the slide and

 this can be dragged into position and re-sized if desired.

More importantly, the sound file itself can be controlled so that it can either be played on demand or automatically.

6f Sound

Controlling the sound

Depending on the type of presentation and/or how you intend giving the presentation will determine how the sound file or sound files will play. The options are...

- Play when the mouse is clicked over it.
- Play when the mouse is moved over it.
- Automatically play when the slide is opened.

Right-click on the speaker icon and choose **Action Settings** from the context menu to open a dialog. The two tabs provide you with control for **Mouse Click** and **Mouse Over**. In most cases you would want to choose one or the other, and in the appropriate dialog, check the **Object action:** button and choose **Play** from the drop-down menu.

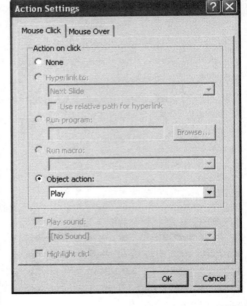

Click **OK** to set the action and close the dialog.

This will set the sound to play in its entirety when the mouse is either clicked over the speaker icon or simply moved over it (depending on which one you chose from the dialog).

Sound 6f

To set the sound to begin automatically when the slide is open, right-click on the speaker icon and choose **Custom Animation...** from the context menu to open a dialog.

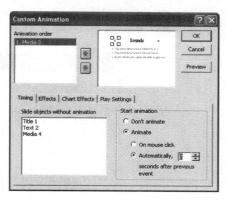

In the **Timing** tab, click on the **Animate** radio button and then the button labelled **Automatically**.

You may then enter a number of seconds after the previous event to begin this sound file. If zero is entered, the sound will begin immediately the slide is displayed.

By clicking the **Play Settings** tab you may choose to pause all other events whilst the sound is playing, or continue with other events (e.g. other sound files, animations, etc.) whilst it is playing.

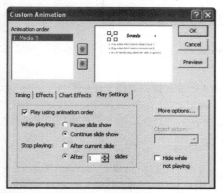

It is possible to have more than one sound file playing (e.g. speech and music) at the same time.

The entry at the bottom left is labelled **Stop playing:** and provides you with the opportunity to stop the sound after the current slide has been replaced, or later. The purpose of this is to stop a sound file which was intended to accompany one slide still playing two or three slides later when its content is not relevant to the slide being displayed.

6f Sound

On the right of the dialog is a button labelled **More options...** and clicking this opens a dialog offering you the choice of looping the sound or rewinding it so that if it is played again, it will begin at the beginning rather than continuing from where it was stopped.

Click **OK** to close the **Play Options** dialog. Click **OK** to close the dialog to fix the settings.

A sound file may be played whilst in the presentation editing mode by double clicking on the speaker icon.

Recording a sound file

Windows is supplied with a small application called Sound Recorder which enables you to record your own sound files (voice, sound effects, music, etc.) The application is usually found by clicking on the **Start** menu, choosing **Programs** (or **All Programs** if you are using Windows XP), going through **Accessories** and then **Entertainment**.

In order to record your own sound, you need a microphone connected to your computer's sound card. You also need to spend some time adjusting its settings so that you get clear sound with a minimum of noise. Right-clicking on the speaker icon on the task bar at the bottom

Sound 6f

right of the screen opens a context menu from which you should select **Adjust Audio Properties**. This opens the audio dialog from where you can make adjustments to the recording and playback, including selecting the audio quality and initiating a test to help you get the most from your computer's sound system.

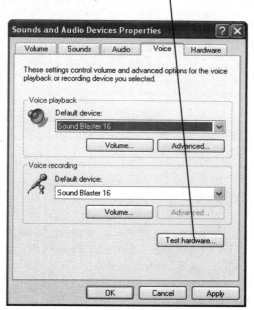

The most common problem users face when trying to record is that of feedback - a screeching sound caused by the microphone picking up sound coming from the speaker which is then amplified, sent out of the speaker, picked up by the microphone, amplified, etc. The easiest way to avoid feedback is to turn the speakers away from the microphone. Switching off the microphone when it's not is use is also recommended, but at other times keep the recording volume to a minimum.

When you're satisfied that you've got the recording playback as good as it's likely to be, including the distance from the microphone to the source of the sound you intend recording, run the Sound Recorder program.

6f Sound

If you intend speaking into the microphone, very carefully prepare what you are going to say. If necessary, write it down and practise reading it a few times so that it is as natural as possible.

The controls on the Sound Recorder window are the same as those you might find on a CD Player or video recorder, except these buttons are operated with a mouse. To begin recording, click on the red **Record** button on the right. When you've finished, click on the **Stop** button which is second from right. To play your recording, click the **Play** button in the centre. The **Fast Rewind** (left) and **Fast Forward** buttons allow you to skip through your recording so that you may edit it.

Although referred to as editing, in reality there isn't much you can do with the recording other than to chop off the beginning and end of the file and combine two or more sound files.

Digital sound recording generates quite large files so it makes a lot of sense to remove any quiet sections at the beginning and end of the file, which can dramatically reduce its size.

Listen carefully to the playback and stop it when the sound begins. Drag the slider to get a more precise position.

Sound 6f

Don't cut it too fine - allow about a quarter of a second before the recording begins. Then, go to the **Edit** menu and choose **Delete Before Current Position** to remove the lead-in section. Do exactly the same at the end, although this time choose **Delete After Current Position**.

To save your file, go to the **File** menu, choose **Save** and save it in the usual way. The file can then be added to your presentation in the manner previously described.

Sound Recorder also allows you to mix two or more recordings as well as adding a file to the current recording by selecting the appropriate entry from the **Edit** menu.

Direct recording

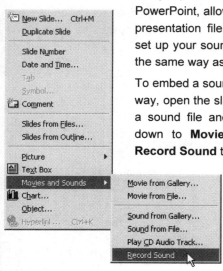

Many presentation applications, including PowerPoint, allow you to record directly into the presentation file. You will, of course, need to set up your sound recording facilities in exactly the same way as previously described.

To embed a sound into your presentation in this way, open the slide onto which you want to add a sound file and go to the **Insert** menu. Go down to **Movies and Sounds** and choose **Record Sound** to open the recording window.

6f Sound

The Record Sound window is similar to that of the Sound Recorder application, and it works in a similar way, but it is much simpler. There is no editing available, just **Record**, **Stop** and **Play** buttons.

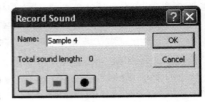

The first task is to give the recording a name and this is entered in the panel at the top of the window. When you're ready to record, click the **Record** button and click **Stop** when you've finished. Unlike Sound Recorder you don't have the luxury of being able to cut off unwanted sections of the recording, so work with care.

You can review your recording by clicking **Play** and if it's as you want it, click **OK**. (If it's not OK, click **Cancel** and start recording again.)

When you have finished, a speaker icon will be displayed on your presentation slide. In the editing mode, double-clicking on the icon should play it. You can adjust the position and size of the icon and add action characteristics to it in exactly the same way as for sound files described on page 114.

Playing a CD

An interesting feature is the ability to embed a command to play a music CD.

You first need to place an audio CD into your computer's CD ROM drive. In some cases, if you have more than one CD ROM drive fitted to your computer, you can put a music CD in each and play tracks from each but in most cases, all tracks will have to be taken from the same CD.

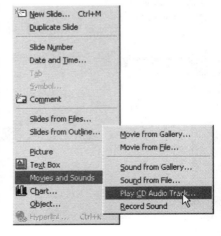

Sound 6f

Go to the **Insert** menu, go down to **Movies and Sounds** and choose **Play CD Audio Track...** to open the **Play Options** dialog.

Not only can you choose the track or the number of tracks you wish to play, but you can also choose a part of a track.

Choose the start and end track by either clicking on the up/down arrows or by deleting the number and typing in a new track number.

If you want to play just one track or a part of one track, the two numbers will be the same.

If you wish to play part of a CD music track you may enter the time in minutes and seconds from the start of the track, and the time in minutes and seconds from the start to where you want it to stop. For example, if you wish to play the part of a CD music track that begins 30 seconds into the track and finishes 45 seconds later, you would enter the start as **00:30** and the end as **01:15**.

When you click **OK** a CD icon will appear on the slide and, like the speaker icon, its size and position can be altered on the slide.

Right-clicking on the CD icon opens a context menu from where you may select **Action Settings...** to determine whether the track will begin with a mouse click on the CD icon or merely moving the mouse over the icon.

From the same context menu you may choose **Custom Animation...** to set up your CD music track so that it can be played automatically when the slide is opened, with or without a time delay and if it is to end when the current slide is replaced. All of these options work in exactly the same as for the recorded sound file (as explained on page 113). The exception is that the **More options...** button on the **Play Settings** tab of

121

6f Sound

the **Custom Animation** dialog leads to the same dialog as shown on page 113 from where you can adjust the CD audio track settings.

Points to consider

- Although sounds can be used in a presentation designed to accompany a talk or lecture, it is more likely to be used in either a stand-alone presentation or an interactive learning module.
- Keep the number of sound files to a minimum if you don't want the viewer to be confronted with a wall of noise.
- If you are using voice recordings, ensure that they don't clash with other sound effects you may be using, for example, slide transition.
- Use the timings shown on the recording applications and the CD audio track set-up to get the sound to play back correctly without overlapping (unless that's what you want them to do).
- When taking the presentation file into a new environment (like an auditorium), you may need to adjust the volume.
- If you are using CD music in your Presentation, make sure you take it with you. (If the CD is not present, it won't stop the presentation from working, you just won't get that piece of sound played.)

6g
Charts and graphs

For quickly comparing data, there's nothing better than a preparing a chart or graph. Providing a visual means to show, say, company growth, is far easier to digest than giving a table of numbers. But a graph can be used instead of numbers in many other situations, not just business.

Types of graph

Before beginning you should have some idea about what sort of chart is needed to display the data. There are many chart types available: some will be determined by the data you want to enter. The main types are...

- Bar and column charts *(comparing values in different sets - eg. ages of a group of children where you want to differentiate between boys and girls.)*

- Pie charts *(where you want to show how something is shared out, like how investment is shared between departments.)*

- Line charts *(where you want to show changing values over a period of time, such as profit on a day to day basis.)*

- Scattergrams *(for comparing two sets of data.)*

You can place a chart on any slide, although it's usually best to begin with a completely blank slide on which to place your chart. If you want to add anything else to that slide it can be included later.

Creating a graph

To place a graph onto a slide, go to the **Insert** menu, and choose **Chart...** which will display a sample chart with a separate panel into which the data can be added or edited.

6g Charts and graphs

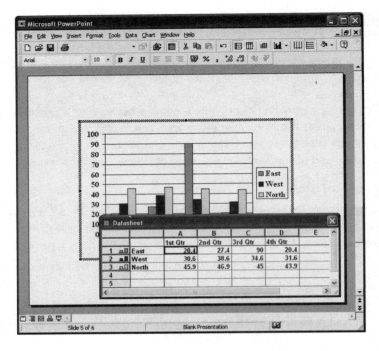

The sample data is unlikely to be of any use and rather than trying to alter it, delete it by right clicking on the button at the top left of the window to select all data..:

… and choosing **Delete** from the context menu.

Begin by entering data onto the table, noting that the row at the very top and the column on the extreme left are for titles and so data should be entered from cell A1 down.

Charts and graphs 6g

Choosing the graph type

As data is entered the graph will begin to be drawn. At this stage you should consider changing the graph type for the one you want. There are two ways to do this. The first is to click the graph icon on the menu bar to show a pictorial menu with 18 graph types. Click on the one you want to use and the graph will be re-drawn in that style. These are just the some of graphs available. To get the full range, open the **Chart** menu and choose **Chart type...** to open a dialog.

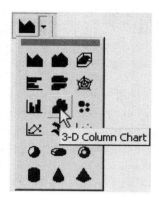

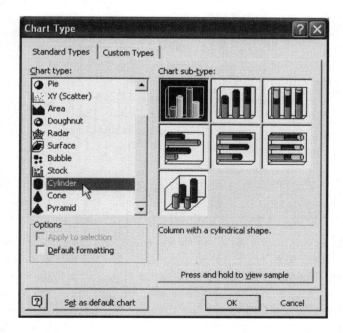

Choose the basic chart type from the list on the left and the sub-type (which can be as many as eight variations on the basic theme) from the

125

6g Charts and graphs

panel on the right. If you don't see anything you like here, you can click on the **Custom** tab at the top of the dialog to reveal a further 20 types of graph covering different types super-imposed on one another, multiple axis and distinctive backdrops.

Graph titles

When the data has been entered, you can place labels in the cells provided at the top of the columns and to the left of the rows.

Further alterations and amendments can be made by going to the **Chart** menu and choosing **Chart Options...** which will open a dialog with six tabs.

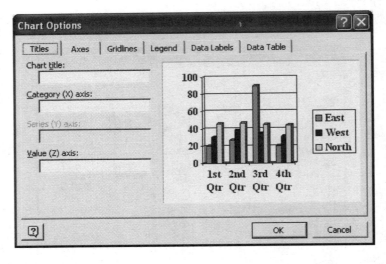

In **Titles** you may enter a title for the graph, and labels for the two or three axes. **Axis** lets you choose how you want the axis to be labelled whilst **Gridlines** lets you choose which lines you want to be displayed. **Legend** allows you to declare where the legend or key is to be positioned, **Data Labels** lets you choose if the data values appear on the chart and **Data Table** displays a matrix below the chart showing the data with the option of including the legend or key with it.

Charts and graphs 6g

Clicking the **OK** button on either dialog fixes the options. When all the data has been entered, the input window may be closed leaving the completed chart on the screen.

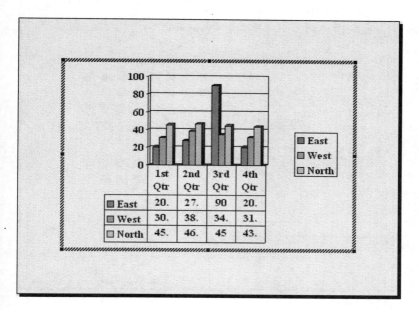

Layout styles

Further alterations can be made to the graph, notably size, fonts and colours.

Altering the size of the graph can be achieved by dragging one of the eight nodes at the corners

The background is, by default, transparent meaning that whatever is behind it will be seen. This might not be desirable as a strong background could make the chart less clear. To colour the background, double-click just inside the frame and a dialog will open from which you can choose a solid background colour and a border for the chart in any colour and in one of a variety of styles.

127

6g Charts and graphs

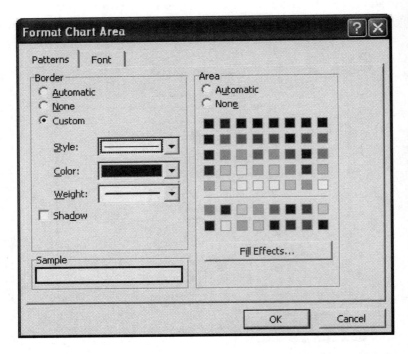

On the left side of the dialog are the options for the border, which by default is set as **None**. Choosing **Custom** will allow you to select the border style, colour and weight by clicking on the arrows at the right of the panels and choosing from the drop-down menus. The options include dotted and dashed lines as well as a solid line and thick shaded bands.

A drop shadow which will make the chart appear to stand out from the surface of the slide can be applied by ticking the box labelled **Shadow**.

On the right of the dialog are the options for the area around the chart and the colour can be chosen from the palette by simply clicking on the desired colour. The sample at the bottom left gives an indication as to what the chosen border/area combination will look like.

Charts and graphs 6g

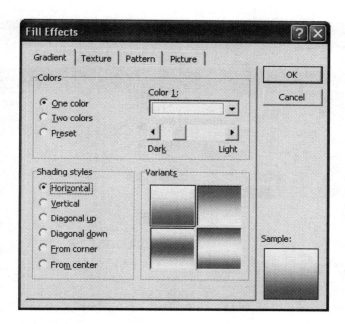

Clicking on the **Fill Effects...** button leads to another dialog with four tabs. In the **Gradient** tab you can choose from a range of graduated fills which can look very stylish. Choose either a single colour (e.g. dark green faded to light green) or two colours (e.g. light blue to black), the shading style (horizontal, etc.) and one of the four variations.

Clicking on the **Texture** tab allows you to choose a texture for the background to the graph. These include wood effect, marble effect and crushed paper effect.

The **Pattern** tab provides a variety of black and white patterns so that you can to print the slide containing your graph on a black and white printer.

Clicking the **Picture** tab allows you to choose a picture, possibly a photograph, which can be placed in the background of your chart.

When you have made your selection, click the **OK** button to return to the previous dialog (shown on page 128).

129

6g Charts and graphs

The other tab is labelled **Fonts** and leads to a dialog from where you may choose the font style, size and weight for the labels which appear on the graph.

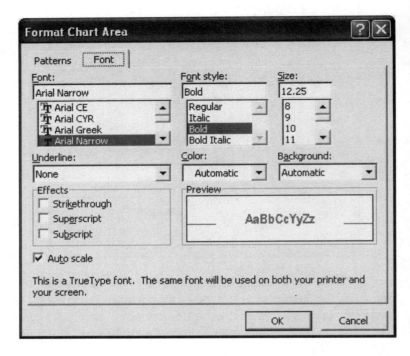

Further font effects available are **Superscript**, which is useful for dates (17th July), and **Subscript**, which is necessary for chemical formulae (H_2O). **Strikethough** looks as through it has been ~~crossed~~ out, and the **Underline** options include single or double underline.

The colour of the font can be chosen by clicking the downward facing arrow alongside the box headed **Color:** which will open the usual colour picker. The **Background:** to the font may be either transparent allowing you to see what is behind or opaque, in which case it will inherit the currently selected background colour.

Click the **OK** button to set your choices.

Charts and graphs   6g

Finishing the chart

The previous four pages describes how to change the background and text of a chart, but the process described actually relates to every element of the chart including...

- Data *(the bars of a bar chart, segments of a pie chart)*
- Grid lines *(horizontal lines showing the vertical scale)*
- Axis lines *(the lines at the bottom and left)*
- Legend *(the key)*
- Walls *(the top and right lines)*.

Exactly which ones will be available for change will depend on what type of graph you have chosen.

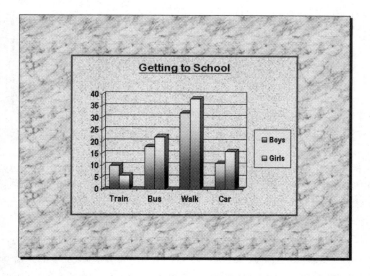

The variations are endless, but remember, these effects are there so that you can make the graph easier to read. Include too many or apply them carelessly and they can have the opposite effect.

6g Charts and graphs

Cut and Paste

If you have a graph which you have created in another application it may be possible to copy the data and paste it into PowerPoint's Datasheet so that the graph can be displayed on a slide.

Open the application which contains the data you wish to use in your presentation, mark the data by dragging the mouse pointer over it whilst holding the left button, and then press **CTRL+C** to copy the data into a special area of the computer's memory called the clipboard.

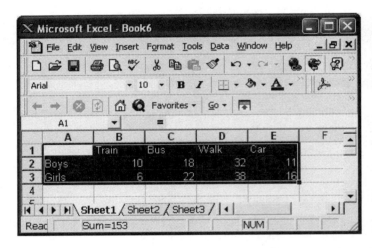

Create a graph in PowerPoint as described on page 123 and remove any sample data from the Datasheet. Click cell A1 and then press **CTRL+V** to paste the data into the Datasheet. You can now continue creating a graph in the usual way.

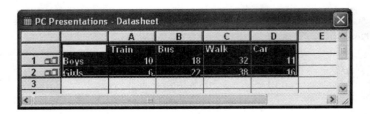

Organisation charts

It is possible, and even likely, that some presentations will need to show how an organisation is run or how a particular business is managed. This potentially complicated information can also be displayed as a chart. These diagrams are called organisational charts and some presentation editing applications feature a built-in editor to help you create one.

To create a new organisation chart in PowerPoint, go to the **Insert** menu and choose **Object...** to open a dialog.

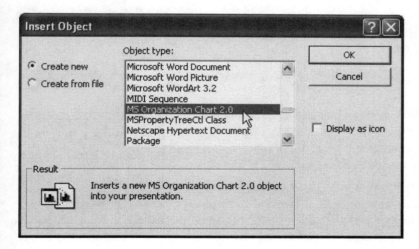

Scroll down to **MS Organisation Chart** and click on it once to highlight it. If you are creating a new chart, click the **Create new** button at the top left. If you are going to use an existing file, click **Create from file** in which case you'll later be asked to locate the file you wish to use.

You can either display the chart as a picture on a slide, or if you select **Display as icon** then just the application icon will be shown on the screen. To see the actual chart you will have to double-click on the icon.

When you click the **OK** button, the chart editor will open with either the previously created chart you selected or a new, blank chart.

6g Charts and graphs

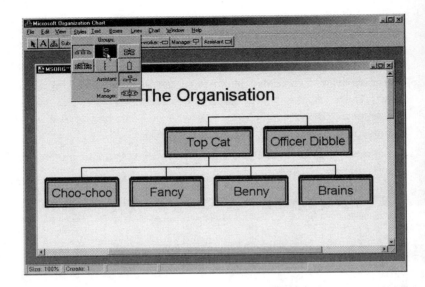

The clever part about this program is that as boxes are added, so the chart rearranges itself to fit into the available space as best it can.

When a new chart is started you are presented with a title and a single box only. Into each box can be entered up to

four pieces of information. Click on the one you wish to insert and type the words. The box will automatically expand or reduce to accommodate the text in it. If a second box on the same level needs to be larger to accommodate a greater amount of text, the first box will increase to the same size.

Most of the box elements are selectable including fill colour, font style, colour and size, frame style and colour and shadow type.

Although boxes on different levels can have different attributes, by default, once a box has been set up, subsequent boxes will inherit the same attributes thus making it easy to create a consistent chart.

Charts and graphs   6g

To add further boxes, select the type of link you require from the button bar...

... and click on a box in the chart.

If the **Subordinate** button is selected, for example, clicking on a box will place a line and another box leading down from the first box. This shows that the worker ranks below the first in order of seniority. A **co-worker** link will place a line and box alongside showing the two jobs are equal. (Referring to the chart below, Benny and Brains are co-workers, whilst Top Cat is senior to both of them.)

The type of chart can be selected from the Styles menu.

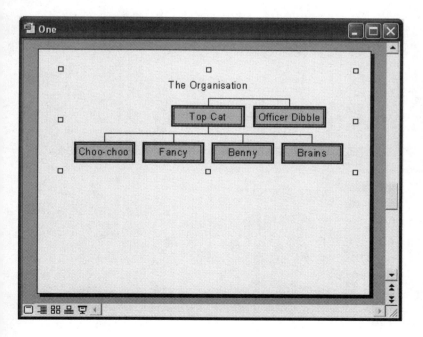

135

6g Charts and graphs

The chart is saved within PowerPoint by going to the **File** menu and choosing **Update**. Should you wish to save it separately, go to the **File** menu and choose **Save Copy As...** .

Once the chart in place, you can drag it into position and resize it using the nodes at the corners or on the sides.

Note that if you want to maintain the aspect ratio (i.e. the ratio of width to height, you must use the corner nodes. If you use the nodes at the sides you will stretch the drawing so that it will look too wide or too tall.

Although the background colour can be changed within the chart editor, it is sometimes better to leave it transparent so that you can see the background selected for the slide. If you want to change to a solid background colour, follow the instructions on page 66.

6h
Other files and effects

Drawing

Not all presentation applications will necessarily have all the features you will need for a particular presentation. As a result, you may need to import files from other applications. Furthermore, if you have a drawing or diagram elsewhere (i.e. in another computer file) you may not want to redraw it for your presentation.

Creating a drawing

There are numerous drawing applications but it's beyond the scope of this book to explain how to create drawings in each one. What can be done is to give an overview of the principle of computer drawing which applies to all of them.

The picture on the following page shows a typical drawing created with a vector graphics application, sometimes referred to as an object-oriented graphics application. Essentially, all of the elements on the right drawing are separate objects which can be moved and coloured individually. On the left is a copy of the drawing but each of the objects have been moved apart clearly demonstrating that each part is individually controllable.

The grid is used to ensure that objects that are supposed to touch, do just that: not overlap or be left with a slight gap between.

The drawing tools provided with programs such as these may seem limited to those who may be used to painting programs. Every drawing is made up of objects that can be closed shapes (square, circle) or lines. Different attributes can be applied to them such as line width, line colour and fill colour.

6h   Other files and effects

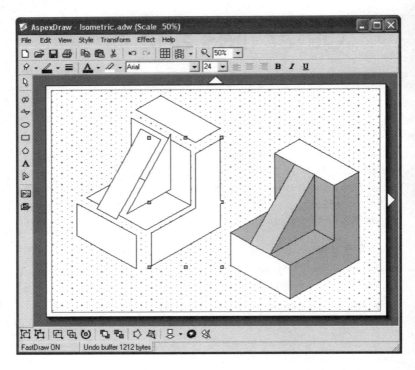

Drawings are usually saved in native format - a filetype specific to the particular drawing application you are using. When creating such a drawing or diagram you should save in native format to ensure that you can recover the drawing in exactly the same state as it was last seen so that it can, if necessary, be altered.

The problem with native graphic formats is that they can't usually be read by presentation applications like PowerPoint. Therefore you also need to save your drawing in a format that can be read by your presentation application. This usually means exporting the picture as a Windows Metafile: a drawing format which can be read by most other applications that are capable of handling pictures.

Other files and effects   6h

Depending on which drawing program you are using will determine exactly how you convert your drawing into a Windows Metafile. In almost all cases, go to the **File** menu. If you see **Export...** or **Export to File...**, choose that. Some will have **Save As...** in which case you must select that option. Either way, an explorer dialog will open.

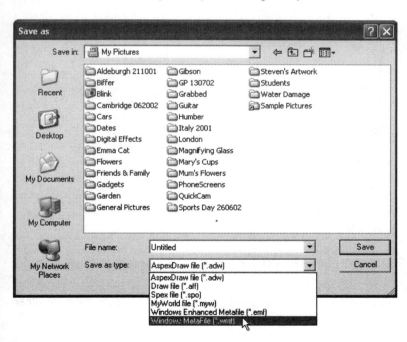

Choose a location to store the file and enter a filename in the usual way. At the bottom is the opportunity to choose the filetype. (The default will

139

6h   Other files and effects

be the native file format.) Click on the downward facing arrow and look for Windows Metafile (*.wmf). The may also be the option of Enhanced Metafile (*.emf). If it is present, it will be worth saving first in that format to see if your presentation editing application can read that filetype. After choosing the filetype, click the **Save** or **Export** button.

Importing the file

The saved or exported drawing can now be placed on a slide in your presentation.

In your presentation editing application, display the page on which you want to place your drawing. Go to the **File** menu, go down to **Picture** and choose **From File...** from the sub menu to open the **Insert Picture** dialog.

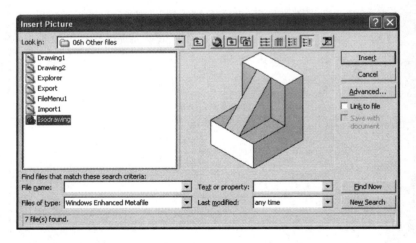

Navigate to locate your file, click on it and a thumbnail will appear on the right of the dialog.

Click the **Import** button to place the picture.

Other files and effects 6h

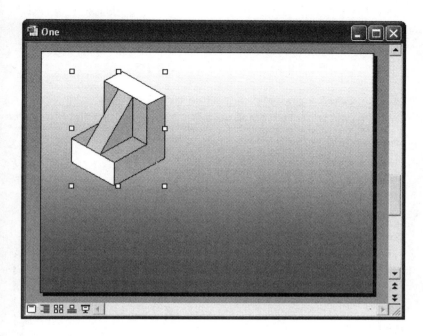

Once the drawing is in place, you can drag it into position and resize it using the nodes at the corners, or the on the sides.

Note that if you want to maintain the aspect ratio (i.e. the ratio of width to height, you must use the corner nodes. If you use the nodes at the sides you will stretch the drawing so that it will look too wide (left) or too tall (right).

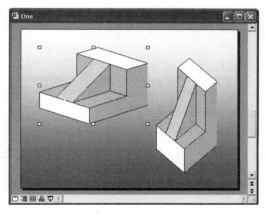

6h Other files and effects

Hyperlinks

Most presentation editing applications provide the facility to include hyperlinks so that you view Intranet or live Internet pages as part of your presentation. Clearly, the computer which you are using to show the presentation must be connected to the Intranet or Internet for this to work.

Any object in a presentation can be given a link. When you have positioned the object, click on it to select it and then go to the **Insert** menu. Click on **Hyperlink** to open a dialog.

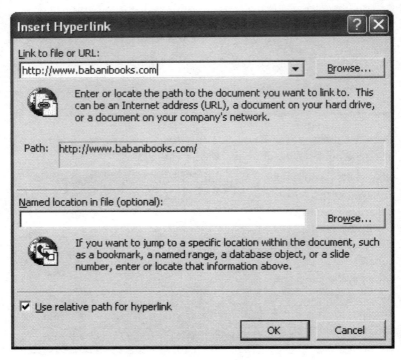

Other files and effects 6h

In the top panel, enter the URL (the web address) of the web page you want to view as part of your presentation and click **OK**.

When the presentation is run, clicking the hyperlink will display the web page declared in the URL.

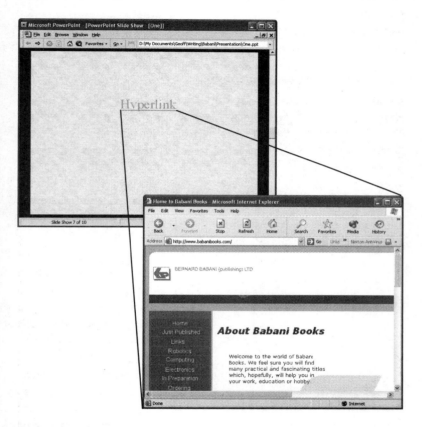

6h   Other files and effects

Launching Applications

Most applications can be launched from within a presentation. The advantage of this feature is that, rather than leaving the presentation and having to search for the application, you can do it quickly and easily with just one click.

There is more than one method of launching applications in PowerPoint. Here are two examples using different methods.

Live camera (Action Settings)

If you have a webcam or video camera connected to the computer you are using to give the presentation, you can focus it on an object and show it as part of your presentation. This would be particularly useful if you wanted to show a small object on the screen.

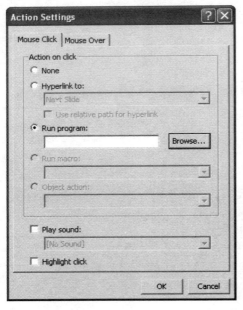

Place an object on the screen, for example a filled square, or perhaps a camera logo to act as a button. Right-click and choose **Action settings...** from the context menu to open a dialog. You can choose to launch an application by either clicking on the button or merely moving the mouse across it depending on whether you select the **Mouse click** or **Mouse over** tab at the top of the dialog.

Check the **Run program:** radio button followed by the **Browse...** button to locate the application you want to launch. When you find the

144

Other files and effects 6h

application icon (or a shortcut to the application you wish to launch), click it once to select it and then click the **OK** button.

The path to the application will be displayed in the **Run program:** box. If you wish, you may click on the **Highlight click** tickbox so that when the launch button is clicked it will change colour. You may also get it to play a sound when the application is launched by clicking the **Play sound:** tick box and choosing a sound file from the list.

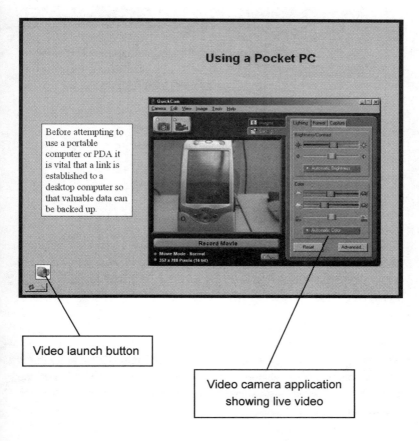

Video launch button

Video camera application showing live video

6h   Other files and effects

MP3 Player (Insert Object)

MP3 files are compressed digital sound files which are usually either downloaded from the Internet or grabbed from music CDs. The advantage of launching an MP3 player is that you will have control over the sound output, including controlling the volume on-screen.

Go to the **Insert** menu and choose **Object...** to open a dialog.

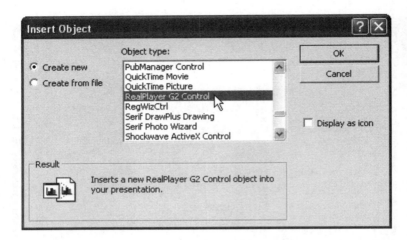

Choose the application you want to launch from the list in the dialog and click the **OK** button. If you tick the **Display as icon** button, then the application icon only will appear on the slide and double-clicking on it will open the application.

Remember, if you are saving your presentation on a CD ROM so that it can be opened on a different computer, you must ensure that the computer on which you intend to run the presentation has the applications you have selected and they are in the same location.

Other files and effects 6h

Organisational Charts

Some applications are designed to link into PowerPoint so that files created in the application can be easily displayed on a PowerPoint slide.

OrgPlus is one such application. It is used to create sophisticated organisation charts.

If *OrgPlus* has been installed on the computer, open the **Insert** menu and choose **Object...** to open a dialog. Click on the appropriate application and decide whether you want to open an existing file or create a new one.

Either way, the *OrgPlus* application will open to enable you to either edit an existing chart or create a new one.

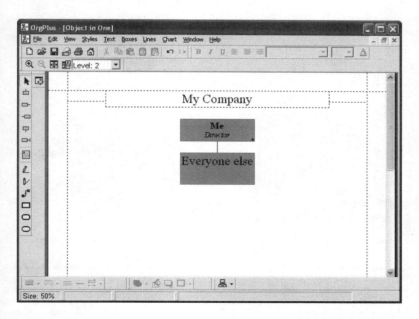

Once the chart has been created, clicking the **Save** button will embed the file into the presentation document. Note, it will not be saved elsewhere unless you specifically want to.

6h   Other files and effects

When *OrgPlus* is closed down, the file will be placed onto the slide and can be resized and positioned.

The interesting feature here is that although you will only be able to edit the chart on a computer onto which *OrgPlus* has been installed, once the chart has been embedded, it can be displayed on any computer, even if *OrgPlus* has not been installed.

7
Special effects

Powerpoint has a wide range of special effects that can be applied to an individual slide, all slides or elements within a slide. Before exploring the range of special effects available, a word of caution: use them sparingly. It's easy to get carried away. If you really want to make an impression, one or two effects are far more striking than dozens on each slide.

Slide changes

One of the easiest ways to improve your presentation is to add an effect to the transition between slides. By default, when you move from one slide to the next, the change is instantaneous, but you can add one of about 40 effects.

Go to the **Slide Show** menu and choose **Slide Transition...** to open a dialog.

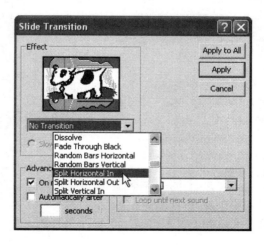

149

7 Special effects

Click the downward facing arrow in the **Effect** area of the dialog and choose the transition effect you want. When you have selected it, the thumbnail above shows the effect by changing from a picture of a door key to a cow.

The thumbnail gives a good impression but sometimes it's better to see it on the actual presentation.

When you've selected the transition you like best, click the **Apply** button to apply the effect to the current slide only, or **Apply to All** to give the same effect for the entire presentation.

The **Apply** button gives you the opportunity to apply a different transition for each slide. If you really want to do that, you can save yourself some time by choosing the last transition option: random, which would normally be applied to all slides.

Speed

Once you have selected a transition effect you can select either slow medium or fast to determine the amount of time the transition effect takes. The point to note here is that the speed will be related to the processor speed and so if you are working on a very old computer, you may find the fast speed acceptable, but when you run the presentation on a newer, faster computer it may prove too fast.

Sound

In addition to adding a visual effect when changing between slides, you can also add a sound effect.

Go to the **Slide Show** menu and choose **Slide Transition...** to open the dialog shown on the previous page. At the bottom right is an area labelled **Sound**. Click the downward facing arrow and choose the sound effect from the list (shown on the right).

150

Special effects 7

If you don't like any of the sounds provided, you can record your own by selecting **Other Sound...** and selecting a pre-recorded sound file. Details of how to do this are outlined on page 115.

When you have selected your sound, click the **Apply** button to apply the effect to the current slide only, or **Apply to All** to give the same effect for the entire presentation.

This effect will be used mainly for presentations that are set to run automatically as it is likely to be an unnecessary distraction when used with a presentation that will accompany a talk or lecture.

Slide effects

The effects relating to how material is displayed on a slide really involves determining how the various objects (either text or graphic elements) on the slide will be introduced.

By default, everything that has been added to each slide appears when the slide is first shown, but you can arrange for objects to appear during the period the slide is being displayed. This can be achieved automatically or under the control of, say, the speaker.

Animation buttons

There is a set of 11 toolbar buttons that control objects on each slide and these are opened by clicking on the yellow star button which displays the **Animated Effects** toolbar.

As with all toolbar components, you can display them on the toolbar at the top of the PowerPoint window (as shown above) or, by dragging the whole bar into the document, as a floating toolkit (left).

151

7   Special effects

Effects buttons

There are eight animated effects that can be applied to text objects, and four that can only be applied to graphic objects on a slide. The group of four buttons shown on the right relate to the effects that can be applied to any graphic or text object. From left to right they are...

> **Drive-in.** The object slides across the screen from the right and arrives in its position accompanied by the sound of screeching brakes.
>
> **Slide-in.** The object arrives from the left (more smoothly than Drive-in) and is accompanied by a whooshing sound.
>
> **Camera.** The object is uncovered, rather like the iris of a camera, and is accompanied by the sound of a camera taking a picture.
>
> **Flash.** The object flashes once on the screen.

The other four effects can only be applied to text objects. From left to right they are...

> **Laser text.** Each letter shoots into position from the top right and is accompanied by a sound that can best be described as a laser gun from Star Wars.
>
> **Typewriter.** Each letter appears on the slide as though it were being typed. Bet you can't guess what the sound accompaniment is!
>
> **Reverse Text Order.** The text rolls onto the screen one line at a time, from bottom to top in silence.
>
> **Drop-in.** Here, each word is dropped into position from the top of the screen, again, in silence.

Each of these text effects takes a considerable amount of time to complete and so should not be used for large blocks of text as viewers would soon become bored waiting for it to appear.

Special effects   7

The buttons on the left of the **Animated Effects** toolbar relate to the title (left button) and everything else on the slide (right button). Clicking the left button will cause the title to be animated in whichever way you choose by selecting the effect from the eight options outlined on the previous page. The effect will normally occur automatically as soon as the slide is displayed, unless other effects have been placed before it.

If the right button is not clicked, all other objects will be on the slide from the time it is it is displayed.

Order of events

The order that each object will be animated will be the order in which you set the animation effect. But you can control the order of events by altering the event number in the panel on the right of the **Animation Effects** toolbar.

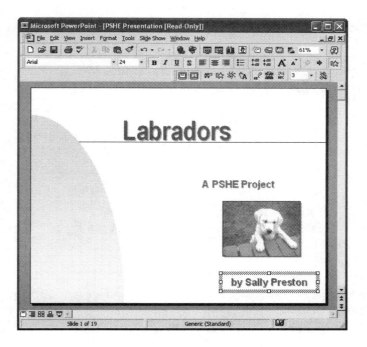

7 Special effects

The screen shown on the previous has four objects - title, sub-title, picture and by-line. The by-line has been selected and as can be seen from the event order number, it is the third object to be animated. To change it to the last, simply change the number in the event order panel to '4' or click on the downward facing arrow and choose the number from the drop-down menu.

To apply an effect to an object, click on the object to select it and then choose the animated effect.

Custom animation

So far, all the animation effects discussed have been applied using their default settings which will be adequate for most purposes. More advanced users might wish to fine-tune the effects.

The last button on the right of the **Animated Effects** toolbar leads to a dialog which give greater control over the effects.

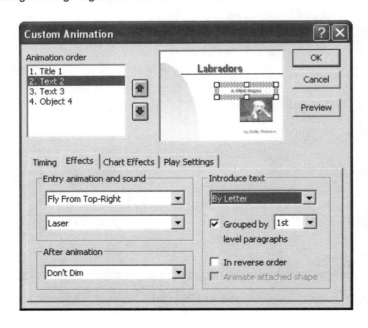

Special effects   7

Animation order

A better way to order the animated effects on each slide is to use the display at the top of the **Custom Animation** dialog. When an object is chosen from the left panel it is highlighted on the right panel enabling you to clearly see which element you are referring to.

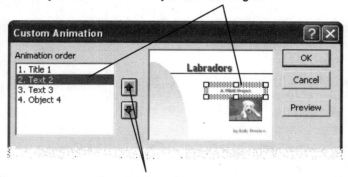

Clicking the up and down arrows will alter the order of the object.

The lower half of the **Custom Animation** dialog has four tabs, each leading to some options which could further enhance the presentation.

Timing

Each animated object can appear on the slide either manually (after a mouse click or pressing the space bar), or automatically. The timing tab allows you to select which you require by selecting either **On mouse click** (which provides manual control) or **Automatically** in which case you must enter the duration after the previous event in seconds.

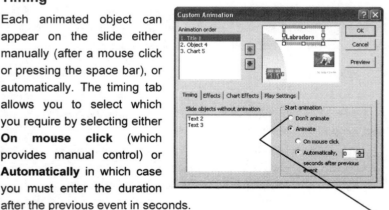

Should you decide not to animate the selected object, click the **Don't animate** button and the object name will be removed from the top panel

155

7 Special effects

and placed in the lower panel. Conversely, the non-animated objects can be moved to the animated list at the top by clicking on the **Animate** button.

Effects

There are several animated effects available in addition to those provided with the toolbar buttons.

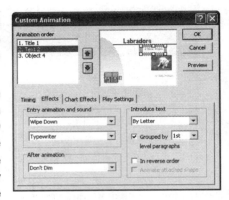

Under the **Entry animation and sound** heading you can choose one of over 40 animated effects from the drop-down menu and choose a sound to go with it. Exactly what animated effects are available will depend on whether you have selected a text object or a graphic object. If you have chosen a text object, then there will be additional options on the right under the heading **Introduce text**. The titles are self-explanatory - you can either have the text appearing on the screen a letter at a time, a word at a time of the whole block of text in one go. You can also arrange for a text object to appear in paragraphs (or bulleted points) and in reverse order.

Chart effect

If you have a chart on a slide then this too can be animated in a variety of ways including separating out the elements of the chart and displaying each element in turn.

You must first declare that the chart is to be animated by going to the **Timing** tab, selecting the chart object from the lower left box and clicking the **Animate** button. Click on the **Chart Effects** tab and on the bottom right under the heading **Entry animation and sound** you can choose the animation effect and the accompanying sound. You may also choose what to do with the chart after it has been displayed. The options are **Don't Dim** (leave it on screen, and continue with the next

Special effects 7

event), **Hide after animation**, **Hide on next mouse click** or **Fade it to a colour** which can be chosen from the list.

The animation choices go further because you can choose to divide the chart into its component parts and apply each component separately, although precisely what is available will depend on what type of chart is being used. On the left is the heading **Introduce chart elements** and below is a panel, initially containing the phrase **All at once**. Clicking the downward facing arrow alongside provides a list of four options. Referring to the chart below...

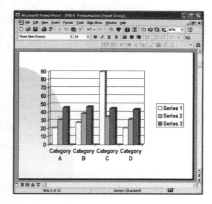

By series. All the white bars would appear first, followed by all light grey bars, then all dark grey bars.

By category. A white, a light grey and a dark grey bar would appear in each category in turn.

By element in series. As with the first option, but the bars appear one at a time rather than all of one series together.

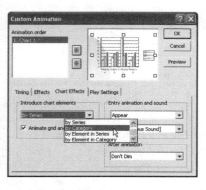

By element in category. As with the second option, but the bars appear one at a time rather than all of one category together.

In addition to these options, you can also choose to have the grid animated separately (instead of simply appearing on the screen) by ticking the box labelled **Animate grid and legend**. This will display the grid first using the chosen animated effect, followed by the chosen method of applying the components of the chart. Note that the actual effect used to animate the grid will be the same as chosen to animate chart components.

157

7 Special effects

Play settings

If you have included a sound or movie file in your presentation then this tab will help you control how and when it is played.

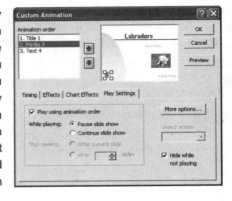

First you must click **Play using animation order** which will add the sound file to the list of animated objects. You can then decide when you want it to begin playing by clicking the up and down arrow. In the example shown here, the title appears first and only after it has appeared does the sound file begin playing.

You can then choose whether you want the presentation to pause until the sound or movie file has finished, or continue running (possibly adding additional objects to the slide) while the file is playing.

If you choose to continue the presentation, select **Continue slide show** which will reveal an additional option labelled **Stop playing:**. This will force the sound or movie file to stop running either after the current slide, or after a number of slides, which you are to decide.

Setting your choices

At any time, you may click the **Preview** button to see what the slide will look like. But be aware that the small size of the thumbnail at the top right of the **Custom Animation** dialog will cause some of the animated effects to run much faster than they would in full screen mode. You may, therefore, have to get it as close as possible with the preview, but do some final adjusting after seeing the slide full size.

Clicking the **OK** button saves the setting and returns you to the PowerPoint editing screen.

Special effects

When should I use them?

The short answer is to use animated effects carefully and sparingly, if at all. In some cases, the use of animations with accompanying sound effects is simply inappropriate. If you are preparing a presentation to accompany a lecture where the audience will comprise professional men and women, then you are not going to want to be continually interrupted and distracted by a string of sound effects ranging from machine guns to screeching brakes. For their part, the delegates are not likely to be enthralled at the sight of lines of text and pictures shooting in and out of the screen in all directions.

But with care and restraint, some effects can actually add power to the presentation. An old overhead projector trick was to use a blind to cover part of the screen. As you talk, the blind is slid down thus revealing additional points.

The slide below has been set up to achieve the same effect. The text is animated with the following settings - **Effect:** *Appear*, **Sound:** *None*, **Introduce text:** *All at once*, **Grouped by:** *1st level paragraphs*.

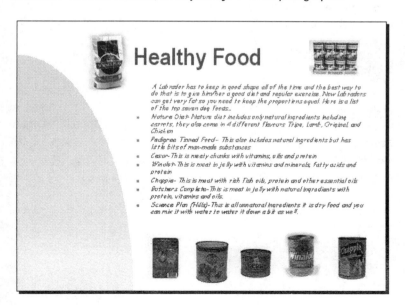

7 Special effects

Each time the space bar is pressed or mouse clicked, another bulleted point is revealed. This means you can talk about each individual point as it appears on screen.

If you are going to use this technique, make a note of how many points there are before you begin. Put the number somewhere in your notes so that you know exactly how many times to press the space bar or click the mouse button before the slide leaves the screen and is replaced by the next one.

Don't try to set up this effect to run automatically. The timings need to be precise to pull it off convincingly.

The only other effect which is acceptable for a presentation aimed at professionals is the transition between slides. If you're going to animate the slide transition use one effect throughout, keep it simple (dissolve or horizontal blinds works quite well), and don't use sound effects with it.

In the classroom

Teenagers will be more impressed with the flashy bits, but don't overdo it here either, because all that will happen is that they will focus on the tricks and ignore the content.

Stand-alone

The place to use the flashing lights and whistles is on a stand-alone presentation (i.e. not designed to accompany a talk or lecture) to capture and maintain people's attention. But even then, use them sparingly. Your presentation should stand up on the basis of the content, not on the clever tricks you've inserted.

In fact, too many fancy tricks can detract from the content.

Display options

8

Computer output

The presentation will be probably be run on a computer which, instead of displaying on a desktop monitor or the screen of a notebook, will be projected onto a large screen which can be seen by all those in the class or conference venue.

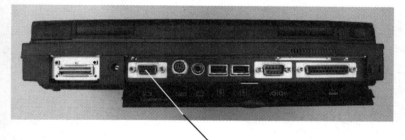

Laptop computers usually have a connection on the rear edge called a video out port into which an additional display or video device may be connected. You can then choose whether the output is to be sent to the built-in display panel and/or the additional video device. When you first connect an additional output device, it is likely that you won't get an image appearing on it until you tell the computer that you want the signal to be sent via this socket.

To choose which video output you require, click on **Start** and choose **Settings**. From the menu, select the **Control Panel** and choose the **Display** icon which will open a dialog in which you can alter various settings relating to the display from your computer.

8 Display options

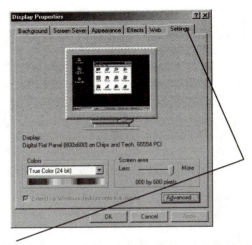

Click on the **Settings** tab at the top of the dialog and then click the **Advanced** button.

Depending on what hardware your computer currently has installed in it will determine exactly what the next dialog will look like. Usually on the top right of the dialog will be a tab relating to your computer's graphics capabilities.

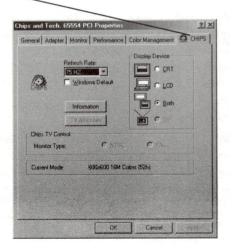

Display options 8

Select this and, from the right of the dialog, you will see an area labelled **Display device**. You will probably find the button alongside **LCD** is the only one that has been selected. Changing to **CRT** (Cathode Ray Tube - a conventional desktop monitor) will send the display through the video port. For presentations, the best option is to choose **Both**. This means that the audience will be able to see what's on the screen whilst you can view the presentation from the monitor thus eliminating the need to be continually turning round to see what the audience is seeing.

Note: If you connect an additional video device to the Video out port, you *may* need to install special software called a driver before you get anything appearing on the screen.

Although the dialog may offer you the choice of outputting the video signal to a CRT monitor, that is not the only video device that can be connected to a computer.

Large screen CRT monitors

Most desktop computers are supplied with a cathode ray tube monitor which is technically not very different from a domestic television set. The size of the monitor is described by its diagonal measurement in inches.

8 Display options

A typical size is 15" although many computers are now offered with slightly larger 17" screens.

The cost of monitors has fallen recently and it is now possible to buy 19" and even 21" CRT monitors relatively cheaply. For giving presentations to small groups (say 20 - 25 maximum) these are ideal. If you want a CRT monitor for larger groups then you would need to consider 29", 34" or even 38" screens although you should be aware that these are very heavy and should not be moved unless they are mounted on a purpose-designed and made trolley.

Like domestic television sets, monitors can suffer from light reflected onto the screen making it difficult to see the display clearly which is why many are supplied with side screens.

Data projector

This is probably the most popular method of showing a presentation to large numbers of people. Like other electronic products, the cost of data projectors has fallen in recent years whilst the performance has improved dramatically.

Display options 8

The first data projectors were not very powerful and the only way you could see what was on the screen was to be in a virtual blackout. The resolution (i.e. the number of dots used to make up the image) was also quite low and so text in particular tended to be a little indistinct a times. This was especially true with smaller text sizes.

Many modern data projectors are now so powerful that you can see the output quite clearly in natural light and the fine resolution means that all of the detail is clearly visible.

When using a data projector, especially in smaller areas like classrooms, it is important to keep well away from screen. In particular, try to avoid pointing to the screen with an opaque object (like a stick, or your arm) as you will cast a large shadow over the screen which will obliterate a large area of the display, including the part you are trying to point to.

You should also be aware that the power of some projectors is such that they are uncomfortable to be near for long periods. Apart from being very bright, they give off a great deal of heat.

Generally, data projectors are placed on a desk but without doubt the best results come from ceiling-mounted projectors which have a remote control to alter the focus. If mounted on the ceiling there is less chance of the presenter casting a shadow on to the screen.

8 Display options

LCD panel

The idea here is that you send the computer's output to a liquid crystal display panel which is placed on a conventional overhead projector. Although the idea didn't really catch on, it led to another idea which is very popular.

Laptop computers have a screen very similar to an LCD panel so someone reasoned that if you've already got an LCD display (which is part of your laptop computer), why buy another? The *Cruiser* looks like a conventional laptop computer but the LCD screen can be removed and placed on an overhead projector. The kit even includes a cable to attach the panel to the computer and a fan to blow cool air across the panel.

Reproduced with permission of Presentations by Design.

The Cruiser requires an overhead projector that is powerful enough to shine through the panel onto the screen. The company also produce a device aptly named the *Toaster* which is effectively a small, portable projector.

This solution is ideal for portable presentations as all you need when you arrive at the venue is a screen onto which to project and a power supply. The problems that exist with the data projector, however, equally apply to this set-up: keep away from the screen and keep away from the projector itself.

Back projection

This is by far the best solution, but you'll only find these at venues which regularly hold conferences as they are very expensive. But the advantage is clear: because the image is projected from behind the screen rather than in front, nothing will obstruct the delegates' view. There is no danger of the speaker casting a shadow onto the screen and as the projector is behind, there will be a clear line of sight between the whole audience and the screen.

Pointing

If you really must point at parts of the display to highlight it, don't use a stick - there are better alternatives. A laser optic pointer emits a bright red parallel beam of light which cannot normally be seen until it actually strikes the screen where it appears as a red dot. But be careful not to point it at anyone as the beam is very powerful and it can hurt if it shines in someone's eye.

Graphics Tablet

If you are proposing to use the pen feature of PowerPoint to 'write' on the presentation display (see page 29), rather than attempting to do it with a mouse (which is very difficult) or trackerball (which is virtually impossible), consider trying a graphics tablet. These devices, supplied by companies such as Trust Inc (www.trust.com/) connect directly to the computer and are supplied with a special pen which enables you to 'write' on the tablet. What you write appears on the screen.

8 Display options

InfraRed presentation aids

If you have one of these tools you can control your presentation from anywhere in the room.

It's basically a 2-button trackerball with the ball and buttons on top within the reach of your thumb. At the top of the handle (in the 'trigger' position) is another button which duplicates the left mouse button, thus enabling you to click the trigger to move onto the next slide without even looking. The device is linked to the computer by infra-red and will easily control a presentation from anywhere in the room, providing there is a line of sight between the controller and the receiver.

These devices enable you to stand away from the screen and control all elements of the presentation, including starting video clips and playing sound samples, as well as moving between slides.

This model by Trust also features a laser beam pointer.

Display options   **8**

Infrared keyboard

To take the remote control feature a stage further, a remote-control keyboard will enable you to add text to the presentation whilst you are giving it.

This particular model features a built in trackerball (the ball is on the top right and the two buttons are on the left) providing the user full control over the display as well as the content of the presentation.

In the classroom, this is a great way to get students involved because you can ask questions and get them to respond by actually doing something, just as they would if they were sitting at their own computer.

The receiver (right) should be positioned as high as possible so the keyboard has the best chance possible to get an uninterrupted line of sight.

169

8 Display options

Interactive whiteboard

Some years ago, touch screen panels were very popular. You simply clipped the clear touch panel over the monitor's screen and a clever arrangement of tiny horizontal and vertical wires enabled the computer to detect where you were pointing. The result was that you could select items simply by pointing to them with your finger.

Reproduced with permission of Atomwide.

Somebody then came up with the idea of making a really large version that is either mounted on the wall or placed on an easel. Onto the screen, the computer's display is projected using a data projector. The result is that you have a large touch screen, big enough for a large class to see, on which you can control the presentation simply by touching areas of the screen.

Display options 8

The use of a whiteboard contradicts several points previously made. In the first place, you will need to stand close to the board to enable you to point to buttons that control the display. Second, you will need to use the special pointer or stylus supplied with the interactive whiteboard and these can cast shadows onto the display. The trick is, when constructing your presentation, place all the control buttons at the edge of the screen so that you don't have to reach across the whiteboard to move the presentation on to the next stage.

Large mouse pointer

Sometimes the mouse pointer can get 'lost' of the screen because there is insufficient contrast between the pointer and the background, because ambient light is making fine detail difficult to see or because the pointer in just too small.

To alter the mouse pointer, click **Start**, choose **Control Panel** and double click on the **Mouse** icon to open a dialog.

8 Display options

Click the Tab headed **Pointer** and from the drop down menu in the **Scheme** area, choose **Windows Standard (Large)** or **Windows Standard (Extra Large)** to increase the size of the mouse pointer. There are also some **Inverted** options (white outline and black fill) that may also be better for some presentation backgrounds.

Whilst in the **Mouse Properties** dialog, click the **Pointer Options** tab.

The visibility of the mouse pointer can be improved by ticking the box labelled **Display pointer trails**. Depending on what device you are using to control the mouse pointer, you may wish to adjust the pointer speed by dragging the slider between **Slow** and **Fast**. This option changes the amount the screen pointer moves relative to the amount the rollerball or mouse is moved.

Whatever hardware or software you are using for your presentation, make sure you are absolutely familiar with its use.

9

Final preparation

Almost ready

By this time you should have decided what you are going to say. You should have the presentation fully functioning, with all material such as pictures and video clips in place.

Speaker's notes

When you have completed the computer element of your presentation, you should think about adding some notes to accompany each screen. The notes would not necessarily be seen by the audience, but are there for you for two reasons…

> 1.. To prompt you in your speaking part. (Very few people can ad-lib successfully. Invariably people who come away after giving a presentation will think of a dozen things they should have said but didn't. Notes will help to prevent you from forgetting important points.)

> 2.. To provide instructions for operation. (Even if your presentation is controlled simply a pressing the space bar to move from one screen to the next, make a note of what needs to be done and where it needs to be done. You may, for example, need to press the space bar at a particular point to reveal the next element of the slide.)

if you wish, add notes to each slide. Click the fourth button at the bottom right of the PowerPoint window and the slide inherits a text box underneath.

9 Final preparation

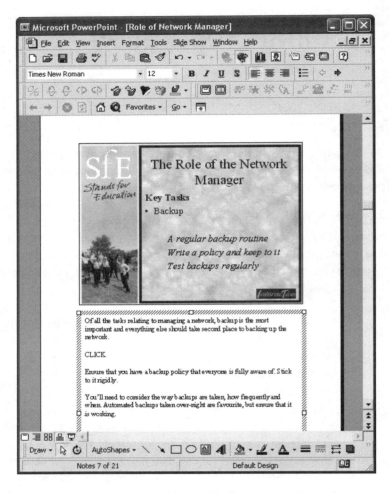

This is clearly a tremendous aid as, with almost no extra work, you can have printed notes, with a picture of the slide at the top which can be easily matched to the slide as it's being displayed. If you happen to lose your thread during the talk, you can very quickly pick up where you left off simply by comparing the displayed slide with the picture on your notes.

Alternative notes

This is a quick and reliable method of creating notes but the drawback is that unless you are speaking from a lectern, you will need to be holding several pieces of A4 paper - one for each slide in your presentation. Anyone who has tried taking an A4 page from the top of a pile and placing at the bottom, whilst you're holding them, will know that this is not an easy feat. If you're slightly nervous and shaking slightly, it's going to be tricky and if you drop them it will be disastrous.

If you can, place the pages on a surface, then this method is fine. If not, and you really feel it will be an advantage having the screenshots on the page with your notes, then staple the top left or top right corner together (whichever you are most comfortable with). At least if you drop your notes they will stay in the correct order.

The other disadvantage of using large pieces of floppy paper is that if you are a little nervous and shaking slightly, sheets of rustling paper will tend to exaggerate the fact.

Many people prefer to use postcards. These are small enough to put in your pocket, easy to handle whilst you're standing and will not flop about in your hand. If you want to tie each card to a particular slide, number them.

Card 1

The Heading
(which should relate to one of the slides)

Point number 1
Point number 2   *(maximum five points)*
Point number 3

You could include some key words with each point, and prompts to let you know when to press Space to reveal the next part of the presentation.

(What the time should be when this slide is finished.)

9 Final preparation

Rehearsal

The type of presentation style you are going to adopt will, to a large extent, determine how much rehearsal is necessary. You will need to do some, even if you are reading a script. If you are working from brief notes you'll probably need more. If you're going to attempt to give the Presentation without any notes whatsoever, you may have to do even more.

Rehearsing a presentation can be a bizarre experience, bordering on the ludicrous, but it is important to do it and it is important to take it seriously. Some people will be more self-conscious during the rehearsal than they will in the real Presentation. But a good rehearsal will enable you to make adjustments to your presentation to take into account any time constraints, but more importantly to help you establish exactly what you will say.

If possible try to practise on someone else. This makes it slightly more realistic as you will be able to get some feedback.

Some people talk into a mirror or make a video recording of their presentation. This feels really strange but enables you to see what you look like and how you will come across to the audience.

Don't over-rehearse. Repeating the same lines over and over and over again, you will begin to get bored with what you're saying and your apathy may come out in the final presentation.

Timing

Depending on the format of the event at which you are giving your presentation will determine just how important timing is. If you are the only speaker, or may be one of two or three speakers, timing may be less of an issue. But remember, if you are one of five or more speakers, each scheduled to speak for 30 minutes, that's a total of 2½ hours. From the audience's point of view, this is quite long enough. If all the speakers overrun by about 30% that will add a further ¾ hour to the time which will be far too long for most people to take at a single sitting.

Final preparation

To under-run is equally bad. Using the same numbers, if five speakers each speak for 10 minutes less than expected, the audience may have to wait for quite a while before lunch is ready to be served.

During the Presentation rehearsal, check how long it takes you to talk through each slide. If you know how long each slide should take, you can adjust the speed up or down to compensate for any differences between what you know each slide should take and the time you are actually taking. If you don't make frequent checks you may not be aware your timing is wrong until it is too late to make any changes.

Handouts for the audience

The audience will often want to take notes about your presentation so that they may refer to them later. Many will bring notepads and paper with them and you will see them frantically scribbling away while you are talking.

If you wish, you can supply the audience with handouts, which feature screenshots of your presentation slides.

9   Final preparation

You can give these out before your presentation, but it is usually better to give them out at the end for several reasons...

1. If you give them out at the beginning it can be a time consuming and potentially disruptive exercise.
2. Giving out notes will probably mean that for the first part of your talk, the audience will be rustling papers because they're more interested in what is on the paper than what you are saying.
3. Giving them a script of your presentation together with screenshots could take away some of your thunder.

To provide handouts with spaces to take notes, open the **File** menu and choose **Print** to open the print dialog.

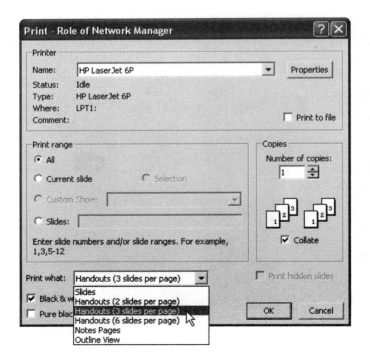

Click on the downward facing arrow alongside the heading **Print what:** to open a drop-down menu from which you can choose the number of slides to be printed on each handout. This also determines how much space there is to write on each sheet.

Remember to re-select from this menu if, at a later stage, you want to print something else.

Questions

If you know your subject, questions should not be a problem although many will understandably be slightly nervous that they could get a question they cannot answer. Spending time trying to predict what questions might arise and preparing answers can be a useful exercise, particularly if you are speaking on behalf of your company and you have a 'company line' to toe.

Nerves

If you're not used to speaking in public, nerves can be a problem. But it may be comforting to know that the most experienced speakers get nerves. (Yes, even me!) In fact, most performers will admit to nerves before going on stage - even if it's to do the play they've been doing every night for the last month.

Actually, nerves are not such a bad thing. They can give us that little extra which can lift our performance.

What is interesting is the fact that we assume that the audience will realise we are nervous, and the thought of that makes us even more nervous. But in reality it's very, very rare that anyone really will spot our nerves, especially if you're on a stage and the nearest member of the audience is 5 metres away.

The two things most people seem to worry about are...

- not finding the right word
- making a fool of oneself.

9   Final preparation

Both are irrational and both can be easily overcome with adequate preparation and rehearsal.

The best way to calm nerves is to stay calm. Being in company the night before may help, but many will find that they do not feel they would be good company and prefer to remain alone on the night before the Presentation. This will provide a good opportunity to quietly go over your Presentation one last time, but don't overdo it. However you choose to spend the night before, it should be a sober night. Alcohol makes us think we are doing better, but actually reduces performance quite significantly. An early night and an early start is usually best.

What should you take?

Having spent several hours preparing your presentation, you want to be sure that when you get it to the venue, it's going to work. Even the best organised of us forget something, some time. It's worth making a list to ensure you've got everything you need...

- The presentation on CD and/or laptop. Take at least two copies - 2 CDs or CD and laptop.
- Fonts, sound files and pictures/diagrams. If you're taking CDs, ensure you take any font files you used with you, and any pictures in case you have to copy the files from CD onto the computer you are using to give the presentation.
- Speaker's notes. Take two copies.
- Handouts. Either enough for everyone or a couple of really good originals which can be photocopied. Many companies will do any photocopying beforehand.
- If you're going by public transport, try to get your ticket the day before you travel or turn up in plenty of time in case there is a queue for tickets.

Final preparation

- If you're staying in a hotel overnight, ensure you have toiletries, a change of clothes and money/credit cards to pay for it if it has not been booked for you.

Also, take a pen and paper and make a note of mileage and fares so that you can claim the costs later.

Introduction

If you have been asked to give the Presentation by a company or outside agency, they may ask you to prepare a short introduction that will be read out by the Master of Ceremonies. This is your opportunity to write a little bit about yourself, in particular what it is that makes you the expert and the reason you've been asked to give the Presentation. If you are asked to do this, it's worth spending a few moments on it. MCs can also get nervous and when they do, they frequently talk and talk because they can't find an easy way to finish. As a result they can actually pre-empt your opening lines.

Usually you just need to jot down a few lines or relevant key phrases and the MC will work them into the opening introductions. Ensure the text you provide is absolutely unambiguous and any names or difficult words are either printed or typed. For example...

- Geoff Preston, ICT Consultant
- Consultant Editor for InteracTive magazine for 8 years.
- Head of ICT for 12 years
- Written widely on ICT issues
- Now Key Stage 3 ICT Consultant for London Borough of Haringey.

Alternatively you may be asked to provide the actual script which will be read out. In some ways this is better as you have greater control on what the MC will and will not say.

9 Final preparation

The introduction should be quite brief and written in the third person...

> I'd like to welcome Geoff Preston who is an ICT consultant and Consultant Editor for InteracTive Magazine.
>
> He was Head of ICT at a North London secondary school where he introduced ICT and where it was routinely used by all subjects.
>
> After leaving the classroom he has written widely on a range of ICT issues and is now Haringey's Key Stage 3 ICT Consultant.

If you have to introduce yourself, use more or less the same script (replacing 'I would like to welcome' with 'I am' and not 'My name is') and put it in the first person (e.g. 'I am' rather than 'Who is'). This is a difficult thing to do because you're in danger of simultaneously selling yourself short and over-emphasising your achievements.

> Good morning. I am Geoff Preston and I am an ICT consultant and Consultant Editor for InteracTive Magazine.
>
> I was Head of ICT at a North London secondary school where I introduced ICT and where it was routinely used by all subjects.
>
> After leaving the classroom I have written widely on a range of ICT issues and I am now Haringey's Key Stage 3 ICT Consultant.

10
Giving the presentation

The big day

The day has finally come, and by the end of the day, it will all be over. You've had a good night's rest, you have a clear head and you've arrived at the conference hall in plenty of time.

Setting up

You may have been able to set up your presentation the night before. If you have, that's one less thing to worry about, or is it. The CD ROM on which your presentation is stored is vital to the success of your presentation which is why I always take two copies. One of which never leaves my side until after the Presentation. If you've only got one copy and it's stuck in a computer overnight which is currently (possibly) unattended, you're not going to get a great deal of sleep.

If you do have to set up in the morning give yourself plenty of time. Many companies will provide technical support for you. All you have to do is tell them what you want and it will be done. Just hand them the CD and they will do what needs to be done to ensure the technology works as it should.

Before the audience arrives, you must satisfy yourself that everything is just as you want it.

Display

Check that the presentation actually works on the computer you are using, which may not have been the computer you used to create the presentation. If you've used any fonts which are not present on the system you are using, you may need to install some fonts. This is particularly true if you've used special characters like arrows which are not part of the 'standard fonts' like Times, Arial or Courier and you have

10 Giving the presentation

forgotten to save the presentation with the **Embed TrueType font** option selected in the **Save** dialog. (See page 25).

Once you have satisfied yourself that the presentation works, make sure everyone can see it.

- If you are using a projector, is it in focus?
- Is the room dark enough so that the screen can be seen sufficiently well that even the smallest text can be easily read?
- Can the screen be seen from everywhere in the room?

If you are giving your presentation in a conference centre, most of these points will have been addressed, but it is as well to check it out yourself.

Controlling the presentation

If you are using your own presentation controller (e.g. an infrared remote-control pointer) check that you've got new batteries in it and check that it works in the hall. Also, check the range. Radio devices usually have a greater range and you do not have to have a clear line of sight between the controller and the receiver. In very humid conditions, some infrared devices seem not to work so well.

Audio

If your presentation includes sounds, you'll need to ensure that it can be heard by everyone in the audience. Run your presentation and go to the back and centre of the auditorium to make sure it can be clearly heard, but remember, the acoustic qualities will change when the hall is full of people. The output from the computer should have a volume control on it: either a physical hardware controller or the software control which can be accessed by clicking on the speaker icon on the bottom right of the toolbar.

Giving the presentation

If you are speaking in a large hall or auditorium you will probably be offered a microphone. If you are offered one, take it. Some will provide a floor-standing microphone which means you won't be able to move away from it. Most, though, will provide a clip-on microphone, and most of them will be cordless 'radio microphones'. On either type, look for the on/off switch and know which is on and which is off.

If you've never used one before, try it. If you have used one before, still try it. You will quickly see how loudly or softly you have to speak to be heard.

The points to remember when using a microphone are...

- As much as possible, keep your voice at a constant volume. A sudden increase in the volume of your voice can sound like the ceiling's coming down.

- Don't tap or hit the microphone accidentally or otherwise. Again, for those sitting close to the loudspeakers it will sound like an earthquake.

- Keep a constant distance from the microphone. This is not an issue with clip-on microphones, but with free-standing versions or those clamped onto a lectern, you need to maintain a constant distance to maintain a constant volume.

- Don't stand too close to the microphone. It's better to stand a little further back and have the volume turned up slightly. If you are too close to the microphone, words containing sounds like 'b' and 'p' will be particularly painful for those close to the speakers.

Some venues will have a sound technician to help you. If possible, practise before the audience arrives.

Technical support

If there is a technician, find out what his/her role will be. Will they, for example, switch on the projector when it's your turn. Will they ensure the computer is on ready for you?

10 Giving the presentation

Final rehearsal

You may have the opportunity to have a full run through. If you do, take it. If you are one of several speakers you may be required to run through your Presentation so that the organisers can be sure everything is as they would like it. Remember, if you've been asked by an organisation, they will also have a reputation to consider and will want to ensure that everything will go to plan.

The audience arrives

You may be in the hall as the audience arrives or you may walk in after everyone is seated. At this stage, your computer should be on, your presentation running and with the first screen on display. If you don't want the audience to see the first screen until you speak, switch the monitor/projector off. Do not have a screensaver set because you don't want the display to keep blanking out during your Presentation.

If you are in the hall as the audience arrives, try to sit calmly. Do not sit reading or shuffling pieces of paper as it will make it look as if you've got something better to do and the audience's arrival is interrupting something which is rather more important.

Look around the audience as they arrive. You may see a smiling face. If so, smile back - you may have made an ally.

Introduction

If there is an MC, s/he will probably begin with some general information and possibly set out some of the 'ground rules' like...

- Coffee will be served at 10:30.
- If you haven't signed up for dinner do so at coffee time.
- The fire exits are either side of the stage and at the back.
- We will take questions at the end.

If you are going to be talking to an audience you have not seen before, you will usually have someone to introduce you. If this is the case you

Giving the presentation   10

will probably have been asked to provide some facts that will be used for the introductions. (See page 181) The introduction might include...

- Who you are.
- Your credentials.
- What you are going to talk about.

Then you hear the words, Ladies and Gentlemen... Geoff Preston. Depending on the occasion, and possibly the lead from the MC, you may get a round of applause. As soon as your name is mentioned, stand up (not jump up) and take up your position. On the way to your position you may need to switch on the projector if there is nobody else to do it for you. You may also need to switch on the microphone.

You're on

Your first actions and your first words will set the tone of your Presentation and could make or break it.

You are the expert, the professional. So act it. There are three things guaranteed to lower the tone at the outset...

- blowing into the microphone to see if it's working
- beginning with an apology
- a private joke between you and someone you know in the audience.

You know the microphone is on, you've just switched it on, so begin speaking. If you can't be heard, someone will know and turn the volume up.

Don't begin with an apology of any kind - it is always a mistake. The message you're giving out is that although the audience have travelled halfway across the country to listen to me, they may have wasted their time.

10 Giving the presentation

If there is someone in the audience you know, don't draw attention to the fact. There's nothing more certain to kill an audience's empathy for the speaker than to listen to chit-chat between the speaker and one of their number. Apart from anything else, it's rude. If you do have someone you know in the audience, use it to your advantage - give them a question to ask. (Making sure, of course, it's a question to which you know the answer.)

Your first words...

... should be Good morning or Welcome or Thank you MC (for that introduction). If you're speaking to the audience, look at them. If you're speaking to the MC, look at him/her.

Humour

Beware of humour. The odd one-liner can go down very well but do be careful not to say anything that might cause offence to someone. A well placed aside or even an amusing (brief) anecdote will put the audience at ease, and if it goes down well, it will put you at ease. But don't let it go to your head. It's very easy to build on the success of one witticism by trying another. Don't, you'll probably be disappointed.

Enthusiasm

You should show your enthusiasm for your subject. This is very important. If the audience sees that you are keen on your subject, it will make what you've got to say more interesting. If you come across as being bored with it, they probably will be too.

Restraint

But amidst your enthusiasm, you must show a degree of restraint. Remember, you are supposed to be giving a Presentation fit for the professional you are and the professionals in your audience. You are not putting on a circus act. Throwing your arms around is not to be recommended.

Giving the presentation   10

Confidence

You must be confident in what you are saying but you must never be arrogant. It's easy to slip into a mode of, 'they've asked me to do it, therefore I must be the best'. If you are arrogant and aggressive, your audience will not warm to you.

Your stance

How you stand speaks volumes about you. Keep your head up and keep your hands out of your pockets. Don't fiddle will papers or pick your fingernails or play with your glasses. It is very distracting. Moving around the speaking area is acceptable providing you're not clocking up too many miles. Above all, do not sway from left to right or backwards and forwards. It can make the audience quite sea-sick.

Involve the audience

I've sat through lots of Presentations and the ones I remember most are the ones where I felt the speaker was speaking to ME. You should try to look at as many people as possible. A good way of doing this is to move your head/eyes in the shape of a letter 'W'. Begin at the back left gradually bring your eyes down to front, about a third of the way in from the left, then to the back centre, then front two-thirds and finally back right. That way you should get eye contact with most people.

If there is someone you know in the audience, try to make a conscious effort not to look at them. We naturally focus on things that are recognisable - in this case it will be people we know. Everyone else can get left out.

Speaking

Work through your prepared material carefully and deliberately. Speak clearly and slowly, but maintain a good pace. If you've taken timings, check the clock occasionally to see you're on schedule, but don't make a big thing of checking the clock. Don't keep looking at your wrist watch either. The audience may think you've got something better to do.

10 Giving the presentation

Questions

When you're asked a question, it's a good idea to repeat it for two reasons...

- the person who asked the question probably won't have a microphone so not everyone will have heard the question
- it gives you a couple of seconds to digest the question and begin to prepare your reply.

Don't immediately jump in with the first thing that comes into your head. It is acceptable to consider your response for a few seconds. When giving your answer, the main focus should not be solely on the person who asked the question. Others may have wanted to ask the same thing. Although you will begin and probably finish your answer by looking at the person who asked the question, don't forget everyone else.

The person who asked the question may then have a follow-up. Try not to get too engrossed with one person. Above all, don't get into a lengthy debate with one individual. If it looks like it's turning into one and/or it's looking like being so obscure that nobody else will be interested, suggest they speak to you after, or throw it to the audience for any responses from them.

Never, ever, embarrass or belittle a questioner. You will get people in the audience who just want to be heard. That is their right. They may ask a question which you've either already addressed or which is so blatantly obvious that you can't think of any sound reason for asking it. But answer it you must, and with the same professionalism you would give to other questions.

Contrary to what many people think, you don't actually have to answer all questions. It can be acceptable to throw the question back to the whole audience or to the questioner. You may not know the answer in which case you could waffle, but it's always better to come clean and say you don't know, but you'll find out.

If you feel the question is more within the field of one of the other speakers, you could throw it over to him/her, but check beforehand that they don't mind you doing so. If you do throw the question to another expert, give them a fair chance. They may be a new speaker who is just about to give their first presentation and is actually concentrating more on their part rather than keeping up with what's currently going on. So, rather than saying, "What do you think?", rephrase the question for them. But remember, if it's acceptable for you to deflect questions to someone else, don't be surprised if others do the same to you. Better keep awake.

Coming to the end

When you finish, go out with a bang. End on a note that will get the audience thinking. Don't finish with a controversial statement and then walk off, but say something to which they can relate. A final nod of the head or a 'Thank you' will almost always be greeted with a round of applause. This may be led by the MC, but if not, don't be disheartened. It may not be the occasion for clapping or you may have just stunned them into silence!

Breaktime

There will doubtless be a coffee break during the morning and you may be asked to have coffee with either the organisers or with the audience. If you're with the organisers, you can relax, especially if your bit is over. If you're with the audience, you're still on duty.

You may be asked about your talk but do not court opinion about it. Your Presentation was just fine, you don't need to be asking people to confirm the fact.

Do not leave the venue as soon as your particular piece is over. You may be asked to take part in a group question/answer session at the end. Even if this is not the case, it is always worth listening to what others have to say. After all, the audience have had to pay to listen to them, you get in for free. Apart from listening to the content, examine the way others give their Presentations. How do they stand? What do they do with their hands? How do they tackle questions?

10 Giving the presentation

It's over

Giving a Presentation is a little like cooking: you spend hours and hours preparing it and then it's consumed within minutes. But you can now relax. Inevitably you will spend some time thinking about your performance - the parts that went well and those that were not quite as good. Don't spend time dwelling on the areas you perceive were not as good. It's unlikely anyone else thought the same, and even if they did, they will have forgotten by now.

It is worth analysing some of it for next time, but for the moment, enjoy the moment and have that drink I said you couldn't have last night.

Expenses

Don't forget to pick up an expenses form from the organisers and complete it as soon as you can, remembering to include all bills for travel and/or accommodation.

Feedback

Most organisers will provide forms for the audience to complete so they can say if they thought it was a positive or negative experience and why. Sometimes these are fed back to the speakers but more often you have to ask.

The responses given by delegates will often be flavoured by the circumstances that brought them to your presentation. Don't take any comments as personal criticism. If there are any negative comments, regard them as food for thought for next time, but above all, enjoy the positive ones.

11
Pitfalls

There are lots of things that can go wrong, but most can be addressed beforehand and need never happen. Here are some classic banana-skins waiting for the unsuspecting speaker to slip on. Each of these has actually happened to someone at some time. (Yes, a couple I put my hands up to.) ...

1. Not knowing exactly what is expected of you in terms of length and structure. You turn up with a 60 minute Presentation on subject X, but it transpires that the audience and organisers are expecting 15 minutes on subject Y.

2. Not recognising that the after-lunch slot (sometimes called the sleepy slot) requires especially stimulating material.

3. Arriving back after lunch ready to give your Presentation, but with bits of spinach stuck in your teeth.

4. Wearing clothes that are so loud that the audience concentrates more on what you are wearing than what you are saying.

5. Turning up with a carefully prepared PC-based presentation only to find the venue has Apple computers.

6. Bringing your super remote-control pointer to operate the presentation but forgetting to replace the batteries which finally give up halfway through your talk.

11 Pitfalls

7. Using so many special effects that are flying on and off the slides that the audience goes cross-eyed.

8. Beginning your talk by thumping the microphone to see if it works which produces a loud noise on the threshold of pain.

9. Beginning with an apology which immediately makes the audience think that they're probably wasting their time.

10. Leaving your mobile phone on and it begins ringing in the middle of your talk. Even worse, your phone is in your inside jacket pocket immediately underneath your clip-on microphone.

11. Using too many clichés like "At the end of the day...". Avoid these like the plague.

12. Not fully understanding the subject you are talking about. The audience will soon latch onto that.

13. Pretending to know the answer to a question that has in fact stumped you.

14. Wearing ill-fitting clothes that need constant adjustment during the course of your Presentation.

15. Leaving your notes and/or presentation material at home or on the train.

Pitfalls 11

16. Referring to statistics that don't actually add up. For example, 60% of the audience are men whilst 45% are women.

17. Opening with a joke that isn't very funny and is actually completely inappropriate.

18. Swaying and/or fiddling with props whilst you are giving your talk.

19. Dropping your notes which are in the form of separate sheets of paper, and apart from not being stapled, they are not numbered either.

20. Not embedding fonts and sounds into the final presentation ensuring that the video clip will be silent and the text will be completely re-formatted.

21. Running through your presentation too quickly so you're left with 10 minutes to ad-lib.

22. Running through your presentation too slowly so that everyone is tapping their feet and the whole day's timetable is over-running. Dinner will be overcooked, as will the organisers and probably the audience too.

23. Not taking the trouble to find out where the Presentation venue is until it's too late to get there on time.

24. Being one of several speakers but not liaising with the others so that they do some of your bits, and you do some of theirs.

11 Pitfalls

Of course, there are some things that can go wrong which are beyond yours, or anyone else's control...

a) Computers and their peripherals do not work well without electricity. A power failure or blown fuse usually brings even the best Presentation to an abrupt end.

b) With lots of bodies in the audience, venues can get hot if they are not air-conditioned. Someone fainting usually causes a distraction and/or disruption which at least might buy you a little extra time.

c) Apart from technical failure due to point a), computers are very reliable but occasionally they go 'feet up'. There's not much you can do about it other than to try and quickly replace the broken item and pick up where you left off. This feature usually brings lots of sympathy/empathy from the audience who will now give you a much easier ride.

12
Quick check

From beginning to end

In many cases, speakers are asked to give a presentation to a group of delegates. When you receive the instructions for your presentation...

1. Research the subject and take any appropriate notes. If you're going to field questions, expect to receive some tough ones so you really need to know your subject well.

2. Write a list of the main points you want to cover. These can be handwritten notes, but if you use a word processor you can copy and paste them into your presentation later.

3. You should also consider any pictures, video clips, sound recordings or animations you might need to include. Start collecting material which is relevant to your talk.

4. Refer back to the original instructions. Have you addressed all the relevant points? If not, make adjustments accordingly.

5. If necessary, modify your notes so that you have not included any unnecessary or irrelevant elements.

6. Break up your notes into smaller, more manageable chunks. It's rather like separating a block of text into paragraphs. These sections will eventually relate to one screen of your presentation.

12 Quick check

7. At this stage you should be beginning to get an idea of what you are going to say. If not, try adding to your notes so that rather than brief prompts, they become more like spoken lines.

8. If you have not been given a software template on which to work, you should create one. Spend time creating a template (or master page as it is sometimes called) as alterations cannot always be easily made at a later stage.

9. Create a new slide on your presentation for each 'block' of your notes.

10. Add key points from each section of your notes. If you find you are trying to fit more than 5 or 6 points per screen, then you should consider dividing your notes up into smaller parts.

11. Don't get carried away with fancy effects at this stage, other than to decide on the font style you intend to use.

12. When you have got all of your screens together, run through the presentation to ensure you've got everything in the order you want.

13. Rearrange any screens that are in the wrong place.

14. If the software allows you to attach notes to each screen, do that now. Alternatively, begin creating prompts on postcards.

15. Run through the presentation again. This is not a dress rehearsal, but simply a brief run through to finally check you've covered all points and the notes (which will form the basis of what you are actually going to say) are associated with the correct screen.

Quick check 12

16. When you are satisfied that you have the order correct and you have covered all points, you can begin refining the screens by adding any graphics, sound recordings and video clips.

17. You may also want to expand your notes so that, if you wish, you can read them as a sort of script.

18. Add any instructions to your notes which will prompt you to change to the next screen or reveal something on the current screen.

19. Print out the screens with notes and prompts.

20. Do another run through, but this time, do it as though it were the real thing (rather like a dress rehearsal) and time it. Follow your notes and change the screens at the correct time. It's worth timing each screen too.

21. You can now expand or reduce what you're actually going to say so that it will fit into a time slot. You may like to alter the notes accordingly.

22. When you're absolutely sure you've got your presentation exactly right, copy it onto a CD ROM or other storage device ready to take to the venue. Take two copies. The organisation that has asked you to give the presentation may also want a copy in advance.

23. Provide the organisation with introduction notes if you're asked to.

24. If you're going to give handouts, get them printed and collated ready to give to the delegates. Alternatively, send a couple of

12   Quick check

master sets to the organisation that has asked you to give the presentation so that they may copy the handouts for the delegates.

25. Make any travel and/or accommodation arrangements.

26. Take suitable clothes with you. Don't forget your toothbrush.

27. Make sure you take your notes, the CD containing your presentation and any additional aids like pointing devices to the venue.

28. Try to have a run through in the venue. Check all the technology works correctly.

29. Relax the night before but don't drink alcohol.

30. Give your presentation.

31. Enjoy the applause and the kudos.

32. Answer any questions to the best of your ability. If you don't know the answer, pass it to another speaker, bounce it back to the audience or say you don't know.

33. Enjoy the rest of the event.

34. Fill in your expenses form.

35. Relax in the bar. You did really well and you deserve a drink.

13
Software and hardware

Useful addresses for software

Several applications have been mentioned in this book. Further information is available from the following addresses...

AspexDraw by *Aspex Software*

If you need to produce quality line drawings for your presentation then you'll need a good drawing application. AspexDraw has lots of features yet is easy to learn. Visit www.aspexsoftware.com/ for purchasing details.

DrawPlus by *Serif*

This title is available in many high street computer shops. DrawPlus is a full-featured drawing program for creating drawings and diagrams for use in a variety of applications, including presentations. Further information about it is available at www.serif.com/.

Office by *Microsoft*

For information about the latest versions of Office (of which PowerPoint is one element) or PowerPoint, visit www.microsoft.com/.

OrgPlus by *Human Concepts*

This program is for creating sophisticated organisation charts. Full details about the different versions of OrgPlus are available from www.orgplus.com/.

13 Software and hardware

Photo Explosion by *Nova*

Sometimes, digital photographs need some alterations to improve their quality or to apply a special effect. This application can be used both for cleaning up digital pictures and creating some stunning effects. More details are available from www.novadevelopment.com/.

PhotoPlus by *Serif*

Full details of this feature-packed photo editing application are at www.serif.com/.

PowerPoint Viewer by *Microsoft*

This application is freely downloadable from www.microsoft.com/office/powerpoint/support/97.asp. It will enable anyone who has a PowerPoint file to view, but not alter it.

Presenter by *Softease*

This simple presentation editor is ideal for learning how to create presentations. Purchasing details are available from www.textease.com/.

Star Office by *Sun Microsystems*

Versions of this integrated office application, which includes a powerful presentation editing application is available as a free download from www.sun.com/.

Video Explosion by *Nova*

Whilst you can display video clips taken straight for a video camera, it is sometimes better to do some editing, particularly between different shots. This application will enable you to create professional-looking video clips. The website is www.novadevelopment.com/.

Software and hardware 13

Useful addresses for hardware

Several useful items of hardware have been mentioned in this book. Further information is available from the following addresses...

Cruiser and Toaster by *Presentations by Design*

The Cruiser is a laptop computer with a detachable screen which can be placed onto a conventional overhead projector and connected to the laptop via a special cable. This enables presentations to be screened without the need for an expensive data projector. For true portability, Toaster, a purpose built OHP is available. Full specifications are available on the website at www.pbduk.co.uk/.

Data Projector from *Atomwide*

This company can supply a wide range of products for presentations including data projectors in a variety of specifications. The data projector is connected to a computer so that the display is projected onto a screen.

Interactive whiteboard from *Atomwide*

Atomwide can also supply a wide range of products for presentations including interactive whiteboards. These enable control of a presentation by pointing at the board.

Large-screen CRT monitors from *Atomwide*

Other products supplied by Atomwide include large-screen cathode ray tube monitors.

13   Software and hardware

Remote pointer/controller by *Trust*

This company produces a wide range of products which will be of use to those giving Presentations. The Trust website is at www.trust.com/.

WebCam by *Logitech*

If you need to include live video in your presentation then a Logitech webcam is a cheap and efficient way of doing it. Logitech's website is at www.logitech.com/.

14
Index

Action button, 55

Action settings, 56, 98, 110, 114, 144

Adding a border, 76

Adding a button, 55

Adding a text box, 65

Ad-lib, 21

Aims, 14

Align, 84

Animated GIF, 91

Animated text, 35

Animation, 91, 155

Audience, 10

Automatic presentation, 59

AutoShape, 87

Background, 48, 79

Capturing from the web, 72

Choosing a graph type, 125

Classroom, 160

Collecting material, 19

Content, 17

Copyright, 20

Creating a graph, 123

Creating a presentation, 23

Cropping a picture, 73

14 Index

Data projector, 164

Delete slide, 52

Digital camera, 71

Direct recording, 119

Distribute, 84

Drawing, 81, 137

Effects buttons, 152, 156

Entering text, 63

Fill effects, 49

Format picture, 77

Graph titles, 126

Graphics tablet, 167

Grid, 83

Group, 83

Guide, 21

Handouts for the audience, 177

Highlights, 92

Hyperlinks, 142

Impress, 38

Improving a photograph, 75

Infrared presentation aids, 168

Inserting pictures, 77

Insert, 52, 55, 109, 133, 140, 146, 147

Interactive learning module, 7, 9

Interactive whiteboards, 170

Introduction, 181, 186

Large mouse pointer, 171

Launching applications, 144

Index 14

LCD panel, 166
Lecture , 5, 9
Lines, 85
Linking slides, 54
Loading your presentation, 26
Location, 11
Lock aspect ratio, 68
Mouse Click, 98, 110
Mouse Over, 98, 110
Movies and Sounds, 113, 121
Nerves, 179
Objectives, 15
Order of events, 153
Organisation charts, 133, 147
Outline view, 27
Page setup, 30
Play Options, 100, 158
Playing a CD, 120
Pointing, 167
Preparing pictures, 73
presentation, 8
Presentation, 8
Presenter, 36
Questions, 179
Ready-made template, 40
Rearrange slides, 53
Recording, 107, 116
Rehearsal, 176

14 Index

Rotation, 95

Running order, 52

Saving your presentation, 25

Scanning a photograph, 72

Setting up, 183

Slide changes, 149, 151

Slide Master, 79

Slide show view, 29

Slide transition, 149

Slide view, 27

Sort view , 28

Sound, 113, 150

Speaker's notes, 173

Special effects, 149

Speech, 21

Stand-alone display, 6, 8, 9, 30, 160

Structure, 16

Television, 108

Template, 39

Text box , 65, 69

Text style, 64

Textual effects, 34

Timing, 57, 155, 176

VCR, 109

Video, 105

Wizard, 43

WordArt, 33

Word processor, 31